D1310499

San Francisco
FIREHOUSE
FAVORITES

San Francisco FIREHOUSE FAVORITES

TONY CALVELLO: *Designer and illustrator*

BRUCE HARLOW: *Photographer*

GEORGIA SACKETT: *Writer*

SHIRLEY SARVIS: *Food writer and consultant*

BONANZA BOOKS · NEW YORK

Copyright © MCMLXV *by Tony Calvello, Bruce Harlow, Georgia Sackett, and Shirley Sarvis*

All rights reserved

Library of Congress catalog card number: 65-26507

This edition published by Bonanza Books,
a division of Crown Publishers, Inc.,
by arrangement with Bobbs Merrill Co., Inc.
h
PRINTED IN THE UNITED STATES OF AMERICA

From Tony to Sandy, Angela, Lynn and John
From Bruce to Merilyn
From Georgia to Chuck, Linda and Mark
From Shirley to my parents

CONTENTS

Tagliarini con Pesto, recipe page 135

It is with heartfelt thanks that we acknowledge the assistance and cooperation of Chief of the San Francisco Fire Department William F. Murray, Deputy Chief William P. Lindecker, Assistant Chief Clarence G. Rosenstock, Battalion Chiefs Fred L. Baumeister and Stanley S. Stojkovich, and the many other firemen who so generously gave of their time to help make this cookbook possible.

The Authors

INTRODUCTION

WHEN A SAN FRANCISCO FIREMAN begins his 24-hour watch, he never knows what to expect—his day may prove full of peril, or monotonous and commonplace. He may be called upon to make a spectacular rescue from a burning downtown building, perched precariously upon a towering aerial ladder, or rush to save a dying heart attack victim with his inhalator. He may begin his day by becoming a common laborer as he goes about the menial task of washdown, clearing away of debris, and overhauling—the systematic search for hidden fire. He may be required to assist in the rescue of a too-daring boy who has attempted to climb the sheer face of rocks at the Cliff House and has frozen halfway up, or he may dash into an apartment blaze on Russian Hill to the cries of "Save my baby!" only to discover that "baby" is a parakeet; if he is a hoseman at the same fire, he will help "send the line along." If he is assigned to Fireboat 1, he may escort a majestic ocean liner on her maiden voyage through the Golden Gate, or he may be assigned the arduous task of transferring thousands of feet of hose from vessel to dock for drying and storage. His practical daily drill may consist of anything from pumper and ladder operations to learning the workings of a new piece of radiological monitoring equipment. In fact, there is only one thing a fireman in San Francisco can count on when he reports to work every third day, and that is his evening meal. He knows with a certainty born of experience that it will be a feast—both of quality and of quantity.

IT SEEMS THAT QUIETLY, with little fanfare, San Francisco's firemen have been grooming over the years, along with the firefighting skills which make the San Francisco Fire Department one of the finest in the nation today, a culinary consciousness which makes them leading gastronomic sophisticates in a city of gastronomes. Since the days when firemen stopped going home for their meals, the city's smoke eaters have been cooking their own food. The result is what is perhaps one of the most talented and least acclaimed pools of amateur cooks to be found anywhere.

THERE IS A SAYING around the Department: "The hotter the fire, the better the cooking." The busiest companies somehow almost always boast the

most outstanding cooks, who are often instrumental in a fireman's putting in for a transfer to a certain company. What has urged this epicurean awareness in so large a group of men, so hardfisted as firemen, and so varied in background and off-duty interests? Undoubtedly it has been spurred on in great part by the fact that San Francisco as a city has always held good food in high esteem. The city houses representatives from every country, who often cook in their old-country style, while San Franciscans taste, approve, encourage, and learn, and ultimately broaden their own world of food.

THE FIREMEN, then, most of whom are native-born, have lived long in the luxury of food carefully and lovingly prepared. 'Way back in 1863, according to a framed menu displayed in the Fire Department's excellent Pioneer Museum, San Francisco firemen were treating themselves to such delights as boiled cod with oyster sauce, herring salad, leg of mutton with caper sauce, cabinet pudding, and at least a score of other delicacies. (The occasion was an anniversary dinner of one of the early volunteer companies.) You can base a solid bet on the fact that the fireman who brews the best cioppino in the Department learned it from a fisherman-father who sailed his fishing boat in the waters off San Francisco, hauling in fresh Pacific Coast crab. The fireman who makes the lightest gnocchi you've ever tasted probably learned the method as a child, watching his Genoese mother mix and knead and cut and poach the little arc-dumplings.

IN EACH OF the city's fifty firehouses, one man each day presides over the kitchen and plots and prepares the food for the day. For all firemen, the dinner hour is the highlight of the day. The firemen pour plenty of thought and anticipation into that moment of eating. Indeed, they all know good food, appreciate it—and demand it. Thus a fireman-cook is inspired to heights of creativity and artistry by his assurance of a knowing and appreciative audience. He may be self-appointed because of his culinary passion or pressed into the position by group decision, where he soon learns the finer points of cookery from scratch. A fireman isn't born knowing how to cook, of course. Occasionally in a firehouse a novice cook can be seen running back and forth between the range and the telephone pleading with his wife, "What do I do now? It's burning!" But all eventually subscribe to the notion that, "If we're going to do this thing, we're going to do it right."

THROUGHOUT THE FIREHOUSES you discover many kinds of cooks —the "down-to-earth" cook, the Italian cook, the *North* Italian cook, the experimental, the devotee of *haute cuisine,* the fussy and temperamental, the good-humored and broadly sweeping, the scholarly. Whatever his approach, a fireman-cook will go to no end of trouble to please his admirers; and will often

French Dressed Cantaloupe,
recipe page 40

dash off to North Beach for fresh basilico or French bread (traditionally, firemen eat no other kind), or to the Farmer's Market for fresh-from-the-country salad greens. Because the firemen must pay for their own food, the cooks watch for food sales carefully, often taking advantage of sales on their days off. One fireman details a man to keep his garlic bread from becoming too crusty. At one house where a lieutenant has "an adverse reaction" to garlic, nothing is ever cooked with garlic. ("We even have garlic bread here without garlic," wails one pained gourmet.) One ample-fronted fireman declares expansively, "I always watch their cholesterol." Another strives for color at his table and insists, "What pleases the eye delights the stomach." Yet another is famed for "cooking down to a gnat's eyelash," so there are never any leftovers for the "other family," or the other watch, to come out of the pockets of the men on his own shift.

THE FIREMEN THEMSELVES are inclined to belittle their culinary skills. "I had to learn to cook; I got married," they'll say, or "Any time you don't burn the food you're a specialist." One fireman insists that his cigar ashes improve the flavor of his superlative Burgundy pot roast. These self-deprecating remarks are typical of the special gallantry that prevails in the Department, only one manifestation of which is that you "never blow your own smoke," or brag. They completely belie the importance of the role the cooks play in the serious side of firehouse cooking, that of morale. High morale is a necessity in a job which often requires a man to risk his life as part of his routine duty. A finely precisioned sense of teamwork, of complete faith in the importance of his work, and in the Department itself, is a must in order for a man to be deployed into hazardous conditions, as a self-contained unit, able to take care of himself and do the right thing at the right time, often working without orders and in silence, for a breath of air may mean his life. The *esprit de corps*, the camaraderie gained in "sitting down together in good fellowship," as one battalion chief puts it, is invaluable in the maintenance of this morale and spirit of teamwork.

ACTUALLY, THE FIREMEN take fierce pride in their cooking and are staunch in standing by their sometimes unorthodox culinary findings: "Never cook a turkey more than two hours; just adjust the heat"; "Never roll enchiladas; stack them"; "Poke the steak full of holes and let the juices run out." Some are highly possessive about their recipes, and one fireman mourns ruefully, "There are only two plank steaks to a side of beef; now everybody in town will be after them."

ABOUT THE ONLY tangible reward a fireman-cook gets for his pains is that he is exempt from having to wash the dishes. He is well aware of the fact that he is courting one of the most critical audiences in the city; in fact, he must be tough-skinned. His lavishly laden tables are often hailed with, "Bring on the dog food," or "Somebody pass me the bicarb, quick!" His marvelous split pea soup may forever be called Prisoner of War Soup or his luscious chowder forever referred to as Kamikaze Gumbo—all this for performing countless hours of kitchen work along with his housework and daily drills, sometimes while studying for a promotional examination, for attention to food can never replace attention to duty. Many a time has a superbly prepared meal placed before firemen just at its prime been left to stand on the table, untouched, to pass its peak, cool, wilt, and die when a fire bell summoned its admirers fast away with its signal of "We roll; first due!"

THESE RECIPES ARE as the firemen cook them. They are dishes men like to cook and men like to eat. But firemen love to "bulk up"; they almost always "pull a second," and so their gargantuan recipes have been scaled to family or dinner-party proportions and then tested without losing their intent.

YOU'LL FIND THIS cook book is abundant in meat recipes. This is a re-flection of firemen. They are essentially meat eaters. They like meat—and the accompaniments are frills. But because they are on a budget, and because so many of the cooks are well versed in preparing the lesser cuts of meat, many of their superb meat dishes are surprisingly economical, as well as innovating. To carry out firehouse cooking, you'll find that a Dutch oven is a requirement. So is tomato sauce. So is garlic.

THE OUTSTANDING RECIPES from the San Francisco firehouses could go on and on—into volumes. Unfortunately, published books have to be of a reasonable size, and lines have to be drawn, and thus many worthy recipes are not to be found in this book. For this regrettable sin of omission we sincerely apologize to fireman-cooks and deprived readers alike.

GEORGIA SACKETT

CHAPTER 1

"jump her lively, boys!"

Brown-Sugared Lemon Pork Chops, recipe page 66

THEY REFLECTED THE very face of American fire fighters of their day—those first volunteer firemen in their proud young settlement of San Francisco. They were aldermen and they were butchers. The tradesman grappled a towrope next to the banker. From the beginning, they were San Francisco's right arm.

THE COMBINATION OF candles and coal-oil lamps and reckless men living in tents and flimsy shacks was disastrous. Six times in as many years was the infant community of gold seekers and adventurers destroyed by flames. The slow processes of building with brick and stone would not be tolerated, and a city of wooden structures arose rapidly after each fire to furnish fuel for the next conflagration. San Franciscans found their city growing to its own peculiar kind of music: the sound of axes dealing blow after blow as buildings which might aid the flames were torn down, the crackling of timber and shingles, and the foreman's shouts of "Jump her lively, boys!" as his crew raced their tiny hand pumper through the plank streets.

THE VOLUNTEERS BROUGHT together by the First Great Fire willingly risked their lives against the same tremendous odds faced by volunteer fire brigades all over the country. The water supply from wells and cisterns was not reliable, so that a fireman might be deprived of his weapons at any moment. Their fire extinguisher, the Babcock hand grenade, a small bottle filled with fluid and thrown into the flames, was effective only in a minor blaze. The watchman at Fort Gunnybags and later in the tower of the City Hall could only guess from which district the glow of fire was coming. But when he rang out his signal, citizens in Prince Albert coats dropped their work to join the red-coated volunteers in dragging out the engines and hose carts, so that the number of hands manning the ropes sometimes swelled to a hundred.

TIME FOUND THE VOLUNTEER companies boasting distinctive characteristics, often with names to match. The Knickerbockers were New Yorkers; the Howards were Bostonians possessed of a fine Hunaman engine. The Lafay-

ette Hook and Ladder Company patterned itself after the famous Parisian fire companies. The Monumentals were Baltimoreans famed for the stream of water their "Big Six" engine threw. No matter what his company, a fireman considered it a matter of pride to see that his engine was first to arrive at a blaze. The engines themselves were often dressed in the most elegant finery. The ornaments of the Rincon Hose Company were typically elaborate: there were mounted eagles, strutting roosters, and flag-bedraped statues.

SAN FRANCISCO'S VOLUNTEER companies were plagued by a discipline problem common to all volunteer fire brigades. Since all rules and regulations were at a company level, the rivalry which had at first stimulated endeavor between the groups began to grow violent. If a burning building bore an insurance mark, indicating a possible reward to those who saved it from fire, any and all means were used to keep the adversary companies from reaching it first. Occasionally a runner was sent ahead to hide the hydrant under a barrel and then sit on top of it innocently while the rival company searched in bewilderment for its water. The frenzied races to the scene of a fire often resulted in a collision of apparatus, which in turn produced many physical battles. Hose spanners, pick handles—anything that was handy was likely to be used for a weapon.

THE INAUGURATION OF the paid Department in 1866 brought a slow but drastic change in firefighting technology. The first innovation was the installation of a fire alarm telegraph system. At first the fireboxes were kept locked, and when a citizen discovered a fire he had to search frantically for a policeman or saloonkeeper who had a key; this shortcoming was soon rectified. The Department boasted a number of ingenious firemen who made important contributions to firefighting methods. One of these was Superintendent of Steamers Daniel Hayes, who built the first turntable hook and ladder truck in the country. Two San Francisco firemen invented the famous "quick-hitch" horse collar which enabled an engine company to have its steamer onto the street fourteen seconds after receiving an alarm. No source of improvement was overlooked. The Leo Brothers, a noted gymnast team, in an exhibition for the officers of the Department introduced a light rope net which promptly replaced the former "catch canvas."

THE STEAMERS WHICH manufacturers developed to cope with the problems of taller, more closely congregated buildings brought to San Francisco the romantic age of horse-drawn equipment. Spectators along Market Street thrilled to the sight of the City's powerful crossed Percheron and English trotters racing to a fire with a steam engine belching forth smoke and leaving a stream of hot

Crab Cioppino Treganza, recipe page 87

cinders. The paid firemen loved their superb horses as much as the volunteers had loved their engines. One horse by the name of Billy was so revered by his driver, truckman Charles Maguire, that he soon came to be known as Billy Maguire.

THE PAID DEPARTMENT was to be put to a severe test of its endurance during the days following April 18, 1906, when the city quivered mightily from earthquake. Within hours after the first shock, fifty-two fires had been reported. Firemen found themselves doubly hampered: Chief of the Department Daniel S. Sullivan had been fatally injured, and the three main water lines to Crystal Springs had been broken. Not until the third day was the fire brought under control by a force of weary firefighters who held the line of defense along Van Ness Avenue for ten hours before they won the battle.

THE AGE OF SCIENCE has arrived in firefighting. But while the present San Francisco Fire Department is a paragon of efficiency, tradition and respect for the past are strong. Scores of San Francisco firemen are both sons and grandsons of firemen. The Chief's car is never called anything but a buggy, from the days when it was horse drawn. Firemen's helmets are as they were when San Francisco was young. There is still much of the romance of yesteryear. One hundred years from now San Francisco's firemen will still be singing "Our Engine On The Hill" as they have been singing it at their gatherings since 1865....

> Come laddies, and draw up your chairs;
>   Let's have a nice sociable time,
> We'll talk of the past, for it may be the last
>   Ere we hear the old City Hall chime.
> But before we begin with our chat
>   Just see that your glasses you fill
> And we'll drink a good toast to the Pride of the Coast
>   Our engine that's housed on the hill.

CHAPTER 2

soups and chowders

SOUPS AND CHOWDERS

In the old days, on the old schedule, lunch was soup and the soupmakers were held in high esteem. (The old schedule was an eight-hour day and lunch was the big meal at the firehouse. With the current twenty-four-hour schedule with a big meal at night, soup is not so vital.)

Nowadays, soup is seldom a meal, but a great soupmaker holds his old-time prestige. Occasionally, one of the "old-timers" can be cajoled into making soup—and that soup is a much-anticipated forerunner to dinner.

Corn-Pimento-Oyster
Chowder, recipe page 25

At Truck No. 13, Bill Killpack is the undisputed soup champion. These are two of his best.

Most firemen lament that this soup is the *approach* to dinner; they'd like to make a meal on it alone.

Cook Killpack says the men like this "cooked up thick—with lots of barley." (Use less barley if you like a lot of broth. Base the soup on meaty lamb bones if oxtails aren't available.)

IRISHMAN'S BARLEY OXTAIL SOUP

2 pounds disjointed oxtails
1 cup pearl barley
Cold water (about 2 quarts)
1 large onion, chopped
2 stalks celery, sliced
2 large carrots, sliced
½ cup chopped fresh parsley
1 bay leaf
1½ teaspoons salt
½ teaspoon freshly ground black
   pepper

Place oxtails and barley in large kettle and cover with cold water. Add remaining ingredients. Heat to boiling, then reduce heat, cover, and simmer for 3 hours or until meat is so tender it falls from the bones. Remove meat from bones; return meat to soup. Remove bay leaf; skim off fat. Taste and correct seasoning with salt and pepper. Makes 6 to 8 servings.

Bill Killpack, Truck Company No. 13

This is the soup course for Friday nights.

CORN-PIMENTO-OYSTER CHOWDER

¼ cup butter
1 large onion, chopped
1 stalk celery, chopped
3 cups water
1 large carrot, thinly sliced crosswise
1 pound potatoes, peeled and diced
¼ cup chopped fresh parsley
1 teaspoon salt
¼ teaspoon *each* black pepper and sugar
1 can (1 pound) cream-style corn
2 cups milk
1 can (4 ounces) pimentos, drained and chopped
1 pint fresh oysters with liquor

Melt butter in large kettle; add onion and celery, and sauté until limp. Add water, carrot, potatoes, parsley, salt, pepper, and sugar. Cook until vegetables are almost tender, about 10 minutes. Add corn and cook 5 minutes more. Add milk, pimento, and oysters, and heat just to boiling; simmer until oyster edges curl. Taste; correct seasoning with salt and pepper. Serve immediately. Makes 8 generous servings.

Bill Killpack, Truck Company No. 13

A lot of carrots give this soup a subtle nuttiness and sweetness. If you wish, sprinkle it with just a few caraway seeds when you serve.

DUTCH ONION SOUP

½ pound bacon slices cut crosswise into ½-inch strips
2 large onions, grated or finely minced
1 pound potatoes, finely diced
4 large carrots, grated
1½ quarts milk
½ teaspoon *each* salt and freshly ground black pepper
3 tablespoons flour mixed to a smooth paste with 3 tablespoons milk

In a large kettle, cook bacon slowly until done but not crisp. Add onions, and sauté just until limp. Add potatoes, carrots, milk, salt, and pepper. Cover and simmer for 4 hours or more. Taste and correct seasoning with salt and pepper. Thicken slightly: stir flour-and-milk paste into soup and heat, stirring, for about 10 minutes. Makes 8 servings.

Frank Noethig, Engine Company No. 48

For years, "Frank the Nut" has been guarding the secret to his thick, sensational minestrone: it's the blue cheese. In the breezy old kitchen of Engine No. 48, perched high on top of Potrero Hill, this minestrone bubbles and builds from early morning until evening dinner.

Serve it with plenty of French bread and butter and it can be supper.

BLUE CHEESE MINESTRONE

2 pounds beef rib bones
Water (about 2½ quarts)
1 cup dried cranberry beans or kidney beans
2 pounds smoked meaty ham hocks, cut in half
3 large carrots, sliced crosswise
1 large onion, chopped
½ cup chopped fresh parsley
1 clove garlic, minced or mashed
1 teaspoon dry mustard
4 ounces uncooked lasagne, broken
1 ounce blue cheese, crumbled
½ pound cabbage, finely shredded
Salt

Place beef bones in kettle, cover with water, bring to a boil, reduce heat, cover, and simmer for 4 hours. Chill bones and broth and remove fat from surface. Add beans and ham hocks, heat to boiling, reduce heat, cover, and simmer for 2 hours more. Chill and remove fat from surface; remove meat from bones; return meat to soup. Add carrots, onions, parsley, garlic, mustard, lasagne, and blue cheese. Cover and simmer 2 hours more. Add cabbage; cook 5 minutes or until tender. Taste; add salt if necessary. Makes 8 servings.

Frank Noethig, Engine Company No. 48

Armenian Salad Platter, recipe page 38

"Prisoner of War" (split pea) soup is a favorite in many of the firehouses, and many cooks make it. Ashley Hobson's is a fine standard.

He likes to make it thick—so you can almost eat it with a fork—and if you like it that way, add another ½ cup or so of split peas to the written recipe. When the soup is all cooked, he uses a potato masher to purée the vegetables and make the soup smooth.

For an Ashley Hobson-style split pea soup lunch or supper, you have to pass a cruet of vinegar for people to sprinkle on according to taste. Also, have hot Cheese French Bread (recipe below).

HOBSON'S SPLIT PEA SOUP

½ pound bacon, finely cut
2 large onions, chopped
3 large carrots, thinly sliced
2 large potatoes, diced
1 cup green split peas
6 cups water
1 can (10½ ounces) beef consommé
  (undiluted)
1 bay leaf
½ teaspoon Worcestershire sauce
½ teaspoon coarsely ground black
  pepper
Salt
Vinegar

In a large kettle with cover, sauté bacon until done but not crisp. Add onions and sauté until limp. Add remaining ingredients except salt and vinegar. Cover and simmer for 2 hours, stirring often. Mash with a potato masher until smooth; or press through a coarse sieve, returning bacon bits to soup; or whirl in blender until smooth. Reheat and correct seasoning with salt, pepper and Worcestershire. Pass vinegar. Makes 8 servings.

CHEESE FRENCH BREAD

Split a loaf of sourdough French bread lengthwise. Open and cut each part into crosswise slices, cutting to but not through crust. Spread with process cheese spread. Sprinkle with sliced green onions with tops. Broil slowly until cheese browns.

Ashley Hobson, Engine Company No. 40

A package of fresh noodles from Chinatown or Japantown makes the base for a quick firehouse lunch soup—served out of deep Chinese soup bowls. At home, it makes a quick first-course soup; but to serve it that way, use a small proportion of noodles to broth.

CHINA SOUP

Put cooked Chinese or Japanese fresh noodles (or any very thin dried noodles, cooked) in bottom of soup bowls. Pour on hot chicken broth to cover. Top with sliced hard-cooked eggs, thin slivers of Chinese barbecued pork (*Char Siu*) (or thin slivers of cooked chicken or ham), and sliced green onions. Offer soy sauce.

Ashley Hobson, Engine Company No. 40

You get a lot of meat in proportion to broth.

MEAT BALL SOUP

1 pound ground chuck
¼ cup *each* cracker crumbs and milk
1 teaspoon salt
¼ teaspoon *each* black pepper, crumbled dried marjoram, sweet basil, rosemary, and thyme
2 cans (10½ ounces *each*) beef consommé
2 soup cans water
2 small carrots, sliced very thinly and cut into shoestring slivers 1½ inches long
½ cup fresh or frozen peas
1 green onion with top, thinly sliced
2 tablespoons dry red wine

Mix together thoroughly the ground chuck, crumbs, milk, salt, pepper, marjoram, basil, rosemary, and thyme; form into small balls about ½ inch in diameter. Combine consommé and water in a saucepan, and heat to boiling. Add carrots, peas, and onions and cook 5 minutes. Add meat balls, a few at a time (so liquid keeps boiling gently), and cook for about 3 minutes or until meat balls float to the surface. Stir in wine. Makes 6 servings.

Cliff Kahn, Engine Company No. 14

Out at Engine No. 23, they say Larry Crabtree is a crackerjack at soup. With a slow, gentle Oklahoma drawl, he'll tell you about his Dust Bowl Soup. The firemen say it's wonderful in the wintertime when it's cold. And it is. It cooks from 8 A.M. until six o'clock dinnertime.

He's thoughtfully blended this soup to the bean-pea family of flavors. He might alter the recipe to permit adding fresh peas near the end of cooking time, but no other vegetables.

DUST BOWL SOUP

2 pounds beef bones
9 cups cold water
½ cup dry pinto beans
½ cup black-eyed peas
⅛ teaspoon crushed dried red peppers
1 large onion, diced
¾ cup chopped celery
1 large celery top sprig
1 medium-sized potato, finely diced
1 clove garlic, minced or mashed
1 tablespoon salt
1 bay leaf
2 teaspoons chili powder
1 teaspoon monosodium glutamate
⅛ teaspoon black pepper

Wash beef bones well, and place in a large kettle with water. Cover, bring to a boil, then simmer very slowly for 2 hours. Add beans, black-eyed peas, and dried red peppers. Cover and simmer for 6 hours more. Skim soup. Add remaining ingredients, cover, and simmer for 1 to 1½ hours longer or until vegetables are tender. Correct seasoning with salt. Makes 6 generous servings.

Larry Crabtree, Engine Company No. 23

Lettuce Buttered New Potatoes and Peas, recipe page 122

MUSHROOM APPETIZER SOUP

4 tablespoons butter
½ pound fresh mushrooms, thinly
  sliced
1½ tablespoons fresh lemon juice
¾ cup chopped fresh parsley
1 can (about 10 ounces) beef bouillon
1 cup sour cream

Melt butter in a large frying pan. Add mushrooms, sprinkle them with lemon juice, and sauté until tender. Stir in parsley and just heat through. Add undiluted beef bouillon. Gradually add ¾ cup of the sour cream. Heat slowly, stirring. Ladle into 6 small soup bowls. Top each with a spoonful of the remaining sour cream. Serve immediately. Makes 6 first-course servings.

Richard Paganelli, Engine Company No. 17

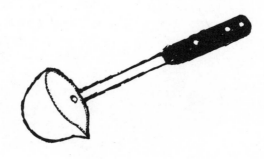

CHAPTER 3

salads

SALADS

Although some stunning exceptions follow, most firehouse salads are tossed green ones. What is tossed with the greens is left to imagination and whim and what's on hand and in season—croutons, radishes, tuna, cucumbers, eggs, beets, anchovies, tomatoes, cheese, artichokes, raw mushrooms, herbs. Except for the oil and vinegar for dressing, *anything* is allowed so long as it tastes right. Oil and vinegar must be the finest—imported olive oil from Italy ("the Italians bring an instinctive distrust of California olive oil"), and fine aged wine vinegar. (Some conscientious Italian fireman brings it back from a Sonoma winery and probably enriches it with pluckings from his mother's herb garden before he gets it to the firehouse.)

Most firemen are pretty haphazard about the proportions for an oil-and-vinegar dressing—and make it by feel. Art Treganza is a precision cook; he has worked out a successful formula and follows it. It's a sharp dressing, and goes well on simple mixed salad greens.

OIL AND VINEGAR DRESSING PIQUANT

6 tablespoons *each* olive oil, wine vinegar, and catsup
1 teaspoon salt
½ teaspoon coarsely ground black pepper
¼ teaspoon grated Parmesan cheese
⅛ teaspoon paprika
About 3 drops Worcestershire sauce
1 clove garlic, crushed

Shake or beat together all ingredients. Let stand at least 1 hour. Remove garlic, and shake or beat again before using. Makes about 1 cup dressing.

Art Treganza,
Airport Rescue Company No. 3

A GREEN SALAD FIRST COURSE

Cut clove of garlic
½ cup salad oil
3 tablespoons wine vinegar
⅜ teaspoon salt
Freshly ground black pepper
4 hard-cooked eggs
6 cups broken lettuce (pack loosely to measure)
Avocado slices

Rub salad bowl with cut clove of garlic. Beat together in salad bowl the oil, vinegar, salt, and pepper. Thinly slice eggs into dressing. Add lettuce and toss lightly but thoroughly. Lift salad onto 4 chilled salad plates; garnish with several avocado slices. Makes 4 generous servings.

Andy Dunn, Engine Company No. 20

The wonderful fresh tastiness of Western greens in a fine salad is dramatized by the Green Dressing Ray Hines concocted for his special salad. (Or you can use the dressing to toss over a salad simply of broken romaine.) Keep any unused dressing covered and chilled in refrigerator.

GREEN DRESSING FOR GREEN SALAD

⅓ cup *each* sliced green onion tops (green part only) and very finely chopped fresh parsley
1 small can (2 ounces) anchovy fillets, drained and minced
1 cup *each* sour cream and mayonnaise
2 tablespoons wine vinegar
Green salad (recipe below)

Mix together thoroughly onion tops, parsley, anchovies, sour cream, mayonnaise, and vinegar. Pass for each person to spoon on green salad. Makes about 2 cups dressing or topping dressing for 8 to 10 salads.

GREEN SALAD

Broken romaine
Thinly sliced cucumber
Avocado slices

Arrange broken romaine in center of individual chilled salad plates. Put a few cucumber slices along one side of romaine and avocado slices on the other.

Ray Hines, Engine Company No. 8

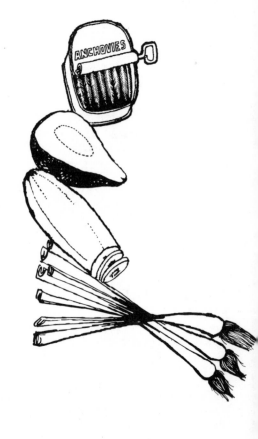

A cool luncheon for a hot day out on Stanyan Street.

You can use the dressing over any chilled fresh fruits. But pineapple is best.

FRESH PINEAPPLE WITH DIVINITY DRESSING

2 ripe fresh pineapples, chilled and cut
    into spears or large chunks
Crisp lettuce
Fresh orange slices, whole strawber-
    ries, and mint leaves for garnish
Divinity dressing (recipe below)

Arrange pineapple on lettuce on six chilled serving plates. Garnish with orange slices, strawberries, and mint leaves. Pass dressing. Makes 6 servings.

DIVINITY DRESSING

Combine in a saucepan 1 cup sugar and ½ cup *each* light corn syrup and hot water. Cook until mixture spins a thread (232° on candy thermometer). In a mixing bowl, beat egg whites until stiff. Pour hot syrup slowly, in a thin stream, into egg whites, beating constantly. Beat in ½ teaspoon vanilla. Cool. Fold in ⅓ cup mayonnaise and grated peel of 1 orange and 1 lemon. Makes about 2 cups dressing.

Ashley Hobson, Engine Company No. 40

A firehouse first course—because it's refreshing. It could be a luncheon salad—because it's hearty.

All ingredients must be well chilled. Make the dressing at least two hours ahead of serving to let it chill and blend flavors. Eaters squeeze lemon juice over the served salad if they wish.

AIRPORT SALAD DE LUXE

½ head iceberg lettuce
1 small can (about 8 ounces) garbanzo beans, well drained and chilled
½ can (8-ounce size) red kidney beans, well drained and chilled
1 small can (about 6 ounces) tuna, chilled, drained, and flaked
2 tomatoes, cut into wedges
2 hard-cooked eggs, sliced
Salt and freshly ground black pepper
Dressing
Lemon wedges

Break lettuce in bite-size pieces into chilled salad bowl. Add garbanzo and kidney beans, tuna, tomatoes, and eggs. Sprinkle with salt and pepper. Pour dressing over, and toss lightly but thoroughly. Garnish with lemon wedges; serve immediately. Makes 6 servings.

DRESSING

Stir together ¼ cup mayonnaise, 1½ teaspoons catsup, and ¼ teaspoon Worcestershire. Stir in 1 teaspoon vinegar. Add 1 tablespoon oil, and stir in thoroughly. Cover and chill.

Harry Humphreys,
Airport Rescue Company No. 1

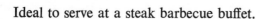

Ideal to serve at a steak barbecue buffet.

ARMENIAN SALAD PLATTER

Line a chilled platter with lettuce. Arrange on it overlapping very thin slices of ripe tomatoes, peeled cucumbers, and green bell peppers. Just before serving, pour on a dressing made in these proportions: Shake or beat together ½ cup olive oil; 2½ tablespoons red wine vinegar; ½ teaspoon catsup; 1 small clove garlic, minced or mashed; ¼ teaspoon *each* salt and paprika; and ⅛ teaspoon freshly ground black pepper.

Jack Kermoian, Engine Company No. 15

AVOCADO CRAB WITH CELERY ROOT

1 medium-sized celery root
Boiling salted water
1 large avocado, cut in large dice
1 pound flaked crab meat
Oregano dressing (recipe below)
6 large tomatoes, partially cut into wedges from top to bottom (or crisp lettuce)
Fresh lemon juice and wedges

Cook trimmed and scrubbed celery root, covered, in boiling salted water until tender, about 45 minutes; cool, peel and dice. Combine with avocado and crab and toss gently with enough dressing to moisten well. Spoon salad into opened tomatoes or onto shredded lettuce on individual salad plates. Sprinkle each salad with lemon juice; garnish with lemon wedges. Pass additional dressing. Makes 6 luncheon salad servings.

OREGANO DRESSING

Mix together thoroughly ¾ cup mayonnaise, 1½ tablespoons prepared seafood cocktail sauce or chili sauce, 3 tablespoons salad oil, ¼ teaspoon garlic salt, ⅛ teaspoon dried oregano crumbled to a powder, and a dash of black pepper. Chill thoroughly.

Herb Muzio, Engine Company No. 44

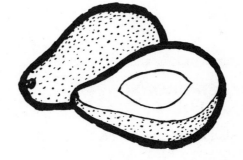

You can make some slight addition if you wish—"a caper or two mashed up and thrown in," perhaps.

FRESH SPINACH–TARRAGON SALAD

1 bunch fresh young spinach leaves, washed, drained, and stems removed
Tarragon dressing
2 hard-cooked eggs, sieved
4 to 6 slices bacon, cooked very crisp and crumbled

Place spinach leaves in a chilled salad bowl, and toss lightly with enough tarragon dressing to coat well. Sprinkle with hard-cooked eggs, top with bacon crumbles. Makes 4 servings.

TARRAGON DRESSING

Shake or beat together ½ cup salad oil, 2 tablespoons wine vinegar, 1 teaspoon sugar, ½ teaspoon *each* salt and crumbled dried tarragon, and ¼ teaspoon coarsely ground black pepper.

Russ McKlem, Engine Company No. 39

A fireman's salad, a lady's lunch.

FRENCH DRESSED CANTALOUPE

2 medium-sized cantaloupe, cut in half crosswise, seeds removed
2 medium-sized tomatoes, cored and cut into thin wedges
½ green bell pepper, seeded and diced
3 green onions with part of the green tops, thinly sliced
½ cup oil-and-vinegar French dressing

With a French melon cutter, scoop melon balls out of cantaloupe flesh; put melon balls into a bowl. Smooth inside of cantaloupe shells and chill. Combine tomatoes, pepper, and onions with melon balls; pour French dressing over. Cover and chill for 4 hours. At serving time, heap marinated mixture into chilled cantaloupe shells. Makes 4 servings.

*Lieutenant Frank Waldeyer,
Engine Company No. 10*

Salad perfectionist Al Boccone on salads: Don't overvinegar the dressing. Don't chill the dressing; that kills the taste. Dress salad *immediately* before serving. Just kiss the lettuce with dressing (don't drown it).

For any green salad, he uses two kinds of lettuce, one hard, one soft, such as icy romaine with velvety butter or Boston lettuce, or resistant curly chicory with soft red leaf.

Toss two lettuces and some little cherry tomatoes with this anchovy dressing. Grind on fresh black pepper.

ANCHOVY DRESSING

¾ cup olive oil
3 tablespoons wine vinegar
½ small can (2-ounce size) anchovies
with oil, finely chopped
½ teaspoon dry mustard
2 green onions with 1 inch of green
tops, finely chopped

Beat or shake all ingredients together thoroughly. Allow to stand at room temperature at least 1 hour before using. Makes about 1 cup dressing.

Al Boccone, Engine Company No. 9

Usually this goes on a salad of romaine and head lettuce, tomato wedges, garbanzo beans, and onions that are quartered and thinly sliced.

BOB HINMAN'S
BLUE CHEESE DRESSING

½ pound Danish blue cheese, crumbled
1 cup mayonnaise
1 small clove garlic, minced or mashed
1 to 2 tablespoons wine vinegar
¼ teaspoon coarsely ground black
pepper
Heavy cream or evaporated milk

Mix together thoroughly the cheese, mayonnaise, garlic, vinegar, and pepper. Cover and chill for at least 1 hour. Just before serving, stir in a little cream to thin to desired consistency. Makes about 1½ cups dressing.

Bob Hinman, Engine Company No. 26

At Engine No. 40, Ashley Hobson puts this zesty cold salad on a lunch menu with Sherried Lima Beans (page 121).

TOMATO SALAD CURRY

6 large ripe tomatoes, peeled, seeded, and chopped
1 small white onion, grated
1 teaspoon salt
¼ teaspoon coarsely ground black pepper
½ cup mayonnaise
2 tablespoons minced fresh parsley
1 teaspoon curry powder

Combine tomatoes, onions, salt, and pepper; cover and chill for 3 hours. Combine mayonnaise, parsley, and curry; cover and chill for 3 hours. To serve, spoon tomato mixture into small bowls; top each with a spoonful of mayonnaise mixture. Makes 8 servings.

Ashley Hobson, Engine Company No. 40

Grinding makes all the difference in the taste of the cabbage; it is unlike shredded. Lieutenant MacCarthy's cole slaw tastes nutty and fresh. He serves it with his Meat Ball Sauce Lasagne (page 136).

GROUND COLE SLAW

1 medium-sized head cabbage
4 teaspoons minced fresh onion
2 teaspoons sugar
About 6 tablespoons mayonnaise
Salt and pepper (optional)

Wash and core cabbage and cut into small wedges. Force cabbage through a meat grinder fitted with a medium blade. (Hold cabbage wedge upright so it will catch in the spiral threads of the grinder.) Combine ground cabbage with onion, sugar, enough mayonnaise to moisten, and salt and pepper, if you wish. Cover and chill several hours before serving. Makes 6 servings.

Lieutenant E. L. MacCarthy,
Airport Company No. 1

Jim Toomey, "The Silver Fox," is the oldest man in the San Francisco Fire Department. He used to cook a lot. Now he cooks just on Friday nights. That is when the men always expect and look forward to his stuffed pear salad; they like it so much they call it his dessert.

Pear halves are sandwiched together with a fat filling of whipped cream cheese, molded in lime gelatin, and topped with a tangy dressing.

CHEESE PEARS IN LIME

8 canned pear halves (about 1 large can, 1 pound, 13 ounces)
1 large package (8 ounces) cream cheese, softened
1 small package (3 ounces) lime-flavored gelatin
Water
Shredded lettuce
Tangy dressing

Drain pears thoroughly and dry on absorbent paper toweling. Beat cream cheese until soft and whipped. Prepare gelatin with water according to package directions; pour gelatin mixture to ½-inch depth in bottom of a deep mold (about 1½ quarts); chill until almost set. Meanwhile, spread cut side of each pear half generously with cream cheese; place two pear halves together in the shape of a whole pear. Arrange stuffed pears evenly in mold; pour in remaining gelatin. Chill until set. At serving time, unmold salad onto shredded lettuce on serving platter, or cut into individual servings and arrange on lettuce on individual salad plates. Top with or pass dressing. Makes 4 large servings.

TANGY DRESSING

Mix together thoroughly ¼ cup mayonnaise, 4 teaspoons chili sauce, 2 teaspoons catsup, and ⅛ teaspoon Worcestershire. Sprinkle generously with paprika.

Jim Toomey,
Airport Rescue Company No. 1

This is for late summer—when the big, ripe, prime tomatoes are in.

TOMATOES TARRAGON

½ cup olive oil
3 tablespoons red wine vinegar
2 teaspoons crumbled dried tarragon
1 teaspoon sugar
½ teaspoon salt
Freshly ground black pepper
4 large ripe tomatoes, well chilled
Broken crisp lettuce

To make dressing: Shake or beat together oil, vinegar, tarragon, sugar, salt and pepper; cover and chill for at least 1 hour; shake again before using. Cut tomatoes into thick slices, and arrange, slightly overlapping, on lettuce. Pour dressing over tomatoes. Serve immediately. Makes 4 generous servings.

Larry Middendorf, Engine Company No. 5

At the fireboat house, B-shift Number 1 Cook Lloyd Lewis makes this dressing to go on a tossed green salad or a kidney and garbanzo bean salad, or this surprising beet and onion salad.

PARMESAN DRESSING, LEWIS

1 cup salad oil
⅓ cup red wine vinegar
2 tablespoons grated Parmesan cheese
1½ teaspoons Worcestershire sauce
½ teaspoon prepared hot mustard
1 teaspoon salt
¼ teaspoon *each* coarsely ground fresh black pepper, paprika, sugar, and crumbled dried parsley
⅛ teaspoon garlic salt
Beet and onion salad (recipe below)

Shake or beat together thoroughly first eleven ingredients. Let stand 1 hour before using. Use to dress beet salad. Makes about 1¼ cups dressing.

BEET AND ONION SALAD

2 cans (1 pound *each*) sliced beets, well drained
2 large onions, sliced very thinly from top to bottom
Crisp lettuce

Mix beets and onions in a bowl and pour over them enough dressing to coat well (about ⅔ cup). Cover and chill 1 hour or more. At serving time, arrange on crisp lettuce. Makes 6 servings.

Lloyd Lewis, Engine Company No. 9

CHAPTER 4

beef and lamb

BEEF AND LAMB

Firemen are big meat eaters; cooks invariably have to figure at least a pound of meat per man.

Firehouse cooks excel at meat cookery: They know meat cuts; they also know the butcher—personally.

This is a perfectly regal beef roast. The standing ribs are roasted rare; they carry a rich cloak of Italian pasta sauce. You pass additional pasta sauce to ladle over carved beef slices.

(You can apply the same treatment to beef roasts less lavish than prime ribs.)

The Italian sauce is Chief Murray's (page 131).

STANDING RIBS DELIZIOSO

3-rib standing rib roast (about 7
  pounds)
Salt and freshly ground black pepper
About 1 quart Chief Murray's Italian
  Gravy, heated (see page 131)

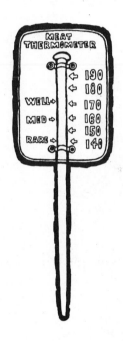

Wipe roast with a damp cloth, rub with salt and pepper. Place meat on a rack in a roasting pan. Place in a very hot oven (450°) for 25 minutes. Reduce oven heat to slow (300°), and roast 45 minutes more. Spoon enough Italian gravy over roast to coat top and sides, and continue to roast for 1 hour more or until meat thermometer registers 140° (for rare) or 150° (for medium rare). Allow to stand 20 minutes before carving. Pass remaining sauce. Makes 6 generous servings.

Jack Sherry, Truck Company No. 3

A visit with Ashley Hobson reveals an explosive "little black book" packed with all sorts of culinary gems—from Chinese Soup to Date Pudding. His titles aren't elaborate—"Chicken," "Good Rice," "Swiss Steak"; they belie the magnificence of the results.

This recipe produces a lot of savory brown gravy; it's a lighter tasting Swiss Steak than most.

SWISS STEAK

2 pounds round steak, cut about 1 inch thick
Flour seasoned well with salt and pepper
About 2 tablespoons shortening
1 medium-sized onion, chopped
1 large carrot, sliced
½ green bell pepper, chopped
¼ cup chopped fresh parsley
⅓ whole lemon, finely chopped
½ bay leaf
1 teaspoon Worcestershire sauce
½ teaspoon Beau Monde seasoning
1 can (10½ ounces) cream of mushroom soup
½ cup *each* dry red wine and water

Rub steak with seasoned flour. In a heavy pan with cover, brown meat on both sides in shortening. Remove any excess fat from pan. Add onion, carrot, green pepper, parsley, lemon, and bay. Combine remaining ingredients, and add to meat. Cover pan; simmer meat until tender, about 1½ hours. Taste gravy and add salt and pepper if necessary. Makes 5 to 6 servings.

Ashley Hobson, Engine Company No. 40

Each beef shank is like an individual pot roast. Serve with hot macaroni and top the macaroni with part of the tomato sauce.

BEEF SHANK POT ROASTS

6 meaty center-cut beef shanks, each at
  least ½ pound and 1 inch thick
Salad oil
Salt and pepper
2 tablespoons instant chopped onions
2 cans (8 ounces *each*) tomato sauce

In a heavy frying pan with cover, brown shanks well in a small amount of oil; season with salt and pepper. Sprinkle with onions; add tomato sauce. Cover and simmer for 1½ hours or until meat is very tender; stir occasionally. Makes 6 servings.

Bob Hinman, Engine Company No. 26

 San Franciscans know "Red-Eye" as the red wine that can have that effect. So a Burgundy pot roast acquired this colorful title as soon as Ed Limberg cooked it for the firehouse aggregation.

RED-EYE POT ROAST

4-to-5-pound boneless pot roast (rump
  or chuck)
1 can (8 ounces) tomato sauce
1 cup dry red wine
2 pieces orange peel (orange part only),
  each about 1 by 2 inches
4 whole cloves
2 cinnamon sticks
1 clove garlic, minced or mashed
12 small boiling onions, peeled

Place meat in a Dutch oven or heavy kettle with cover. Combine tomato sauce and ½ cup of the wine and add to meat along with orange peel, cloves, cinnamon, and garlic. Cover and place in a slow oven (300°) for 3 hours. Add remaining wine and onions. Cover and cook 1 hour longer or until onions and meat are tender. Remove meat and let stand a few minutes before slicing. Skim excess fat off juices. Serve juices as sauce over meat slices. (Thicken juices if you wish with a cornstarch-and-water paste.) Makes 6 to 8 servings.

Ed Limberg, Engine Company No. 21

Frank Alianza is a master at blending foreign dishes. He likes to put together what he likes best in one national cuisine with what he likes best in another. Here he combines the crisp green onions of Japanese Sukiyaki with the meat and saucing of Russian Stroganoff.

SUKIYAKI STROGANOFF

1 pound top round steak, sliced very thin and cut into 3-inch lengths
4 tablespoons salad oil
1 medium-sized onion, finely chopped
½ teaspoon salt
⅛ teaspoon pepper
¾ cup dry white table wine
½ can (10½-ounce size) cream of chicken soup, undiluted
¼ pound fresh mushrooms, sliced
1 cup sour cream
¼ cup green onion tops cut in 1½-inch lengths
Steamed white rice

In a large frying pan, sauté beef quickly in salad oil until well browned. Add onions, and sauté just until limp. Stir in salt, pepper, and ½ cup of the wine. Stir in chicken soup. Cook gently, uncovered, stirring occasionally, until meat is tender, about 15 minutes. Stir in remaining wine and mushrooms and cook 5 minutes more or until mushrooms are tender. Reduce heat. Stir in sour cream and green onion tops, and just heat through (do not boil). Serve over rice. Makes 4 servings.

Frank Alianza, Engine Company No. 1

It takes a while to make these, but don't despair; the results are well worth the time.

Armenian Bill Penirian learned from his mother how to make these stuffed grape leaves. Somehow, now that the dish has become known at Engine No. 23, it's undergone a title change.

ARMENIAN GRAPE LEAF MEAT BALLS

2 pounds ground chuck
1 medium-sized onion, very finely chopped
1 egg, slightly beaten
1 teaspoon salt
⅜ teaspoon coarsely ground fresh black pepper
¼ cup long grain white rice
2 tablespoons *each* very finely chopped green bell pepper and fresh parsley
1 quart jar grape leaves
Cold water (about 1 cup)
1 large can (15 ounces) tomato sauce
½ teaspoon crumbled dried oregano
1 clove garlic, minced or mashed
1 tablespoon fresh lemon juice
Yogurt

Mix thoroughly the chuck, onion, egg, salt, pepper, 2 tablespoons of the rice, bell pepper, and parsley. Cut stems off grape leaves if necessary, and rinse

leaves well in cool water. Pinch off a walnut-size piece (or smaller, depending on size of grape leaf; the meat should be enclosed in grape leaf) of the meat mixture. Form into a little log shape and place at base of grape leaf. Roll up, folding in ends of leaf to make a firm packet. Place in a kettle (about 3-quart size) with tight-fitting cover. Repeat, using all meat mixture and grape leaves, and stacking the little rolls close together and several layers deep in kettle. Add cold water to reach almost to top of rolls. Add tomato sauce, oregano, garlic, lemon juice, remaining rice, and any remaining grape leaves. Stir sauce slightly (don't disturb rolls). Cover, bring to boiling point, then simmer for 45 minutes or until rice is tender. To serve, spoon meat rolls in sauce onto plates, top with yogurt. Makes 8 servings.

Bill Penirian, Engine Company No. 23

Fresh herbs and garlic, minced together to a paste, tucked under the fat tied around a rolled beef roast—and the fresh herb flavors penetrate deep into the meat as it sears and roasts. The roast juices and vegetables become a rich sauce for meat slices or accompanying pasta.

HERB BORDERED ITALIC ROAST

¼ cup chopped fresh parsley
Leaves from 3 sprigs fresh rosemary
2 large cloves garlic, peeled
Salt and pepper
5-pound rolled sirloin butt or rib beef roast
Olive oil
2 stalks celery, cut into thirds
2 carrots, peeled, and cut into thirds
2 onions, quartered
2 cloves garlic (unpeeled)
½ green bell pepper, chopped
About 1 cup beef broth
⅔ cup dry red wine

Mince together parsley, rosemary, two cloves garlic, ½ teaspoon salt, and ¹⁄₁₆ teaspoon pepper almost to a paste; tuck under fat layer tied around roast. Rub surface of meat with salt and pepper. In a large heavy frying pan or Dutch oven, brown meat very well on all sides in a small amount of olive oil. Pour off accumulated fat. Add to meat the celery, carrots, onions, unpeeled garlic, bell pepper, 1 cup beef broth, and all but 2 tablespoons of the wine. Cook, uncovered, in a moderate oven (350°) for 1½ hours or until meat is tender; turn roast every 15 minutes. Remove meat to carving board, and allow to stand 15 minutes before carving.

Remove vegetables from pan juices, discard garlic, and whirl remainder in a blender or press through a sieve to purée. Skim fat from meat juices; add puréed vegetables, remaining wine, and enough beef broth to thin to desired sauce consistency. Heat, stirring, to blend. Correct seasoning with salt and pepper. Makes 10 servings.

Dick Marracq, Engine Company No. 34

No firehouse exists without a corned beef dinner occasionally. It is real fireman's fare. Many cooks like to make it; probably every fireman loves to eat it.

James Dowling (they say he looks like Santa) is one of those down-to-earth cooks who does an excellent corned beef (as well as roasts, leg of lamb, chops, anything he cooks). He says his corned beef is like everybody else's—but it's not. His touch and accompaniments make the difference.

STANYAN STREET CORNED BEEF AND CABBAGE

Cook corned beef (brisket or bottom round) as usual, seasoning cooking water with bay, whole cloves, onion, and garlic. When meat is very tender, remove to carving board.

Bring water in which beef cooked to a full rolling boil, and add inch-thick cabbage wedges, a few at a time (so water keeps boiling). Cover, and cook at a full rolling boil for 10 minutes or until cabbage is tender. Drain, chop coarsely, and season with finely sliced green onions, butter, salt, and pepper. Slice corned beef and serve hot.

Accompany with: Homemade beer mustard (stir beer into dry mustard, a little at a time, to make a smooth paste; salt to taste)
Parsleyed new potatoes
Chilled tart applesauce spiced with a little cinnamon
Rye bread and butter

James Dowling, Engine Company No. 40

It used to be a fireman could have a leg of lamb corned, just by asking his butcher to put it into his corning brine. That's how John Griffin used to begin preparation of his Pickled Lamb. He'd have the butcher put a leg of lamb into the brine on Wednesday, take it out on Saturday. Now you may be able to do the same thing if you have a *very* agreeable butcher with a continuing corning brine. But you can do the corning yourself and still accomplish the flavor of that old-fashioned Pickled Lamb that John Griffin used to make. The currant mustard that goes with it is a must. (You can also use the sauce on slices of roast fresh lamb.)

CORNED LEG OF LAMB WITH CURRANT MUSTARD

To corn a leg of lamb yourself:

Purchase a 5-to-6-pound leg of lamb, and have it boned, rolled, and tied. Wipe meat clean with a damp cloth and, with a metal skewer, punch holes deep into meat on all sides. Place in an earthenware, enamel, glass, or plastic container. Pour in corning brine (recipe below) to cover meat by an inch. Place a clean plate on meat, and place a weight on the plate to keep the meat submerged. Refrigerate for 4 days; turn meat over after 2 days. After curing, rinse well in cool water.

Corning brine:

In a large container, combine 1¼ cups rock salt or ice cream salt; 1 cup brown sugar, firmly packed; ¾ teaspoon baking soda; and 2 teaspoons powdered saltpeter (available in drugstores). Pour 1 quart lukewarm water over salt mixture, and stir until thoroughly dissolved. Add 1 quart cold water.

To cook corned lamb:

Place meat in kettle, cover with cold water. Cover and bring to a boil, then simmer for 3 hours or until meat is tender. Add 4 whole carrots and 4 medium-sized whole onions. Simmer 30 minutes more or until vegetables are tender. Remove meat from cooking liquid, and allow to stand about 10 minutes before carving. Serve meat and vegetables with currant mustard (below). Makes 8 servings.

Currant mustard:

Slowly heat 1 cup red currant jelly, stirring, until it melts. Stir in 2 teaspoons Dijon-style prepared mustard until thoroughly blended. Serve hot.

Lieutenant John Griffin,
Engine Company No. 42

Created especially for days when the firehouse budget is slim.

BILL MOELLER'S BREAST OF LAMB

6 to 8 pounds breast of lamb
1 large onion, chopped
4 large cloves garlic, minced or mashed
1 can (14½ ounces) evaporated milk
2 eggs, beaten
2 bay leaves
1 tablespoon crumbled dried oregano
1 teaspoon salt
½ teaspoon pepper
Cracker meal
2 or 3 cans (10¾ ounces *each*) cream
   of tomato soup diluted with 1 or 1½
   soup cans water
Hot steamed rice

Cut lamb into 2- or 3-riblet pieces; remove all excess fat. Combine onion, garlic, milk, eggs, bay leaves, oregano, salt, and pepper in a large bowl. Add lamb, and marinate at room temperature for 2 hours. Roll each lamb piece in cracker meal, and place, bone side down, in a single layer in a shallow greased baking pan. Bake in a slow oven (325°) for 2 hours; turn once.

Meantime, combine soup and water and bring to a boil. Drain excess fat off baked lamb. Pour tomato sauce over lamb. Reduce oven heat to 300°; bake lamb 15 minutes more. Serve with rice, spooning tomato sauce over lamb and rice. Makes 4 to 6 servings.

Note: For 6 pounds of meat, use 2 cans soup for sauce, and plan to serve 4 people; for 8 pounds meat, use 3 cans soup, and expect to serve 6.

Bill Moeller, Truck Company No. 18

Al Boccone borrows the scaloppine technique from veal, and makes it the finish for roasted lamb shanks.

SCALOPPINE LAMB SHANKS

4 lamb shanks
Salt and pepper
1 cup water
½ cup Marsala wine
½ pound fresh mushrooms, sliced
¼ cup *each* sliced green onions with part of the tops and chopped fresh parsley
1 small clove garlic, minced or mashed
¼ teaspoon crumbled dried rosemary

Season lamb shanks with salt and pepper. Place in a greased baking pan. Bake in a moderate oven (350°) for 1 hour or until browned; turn once. Pour off accumulated fat. Pour half the water and half the Marsala over lamb, cover, and bake 1 hour more. Sprinkle lamb with mushrooms, green onions, and parsley. Combine remaining water and wine, garlic, and rosemary; pour over lamb. Cover and bake in a hot oven (400°) for 30 minutes more or until lamb is very tender. Makes 4 servings.

Al Boccone, Engine Company No. 9

CHAPTER 5

veal and pork

VEAL AND PORK

Many Italian cooks choose veal. And several proud firehouses stake their claim to food fame solely on the veal expertise of one talented Italian cook in the house—and his Veal Parmigiana or Scaloppine or stew.

Pork seems international—as witness a Frenchman's sausage-stuffed pork roast, Chinese sweet-and-sour sauced spareribs, Paprika Pork with the influence of Hungary, all-American pork chops . . .

"If anything's worth cooking, it's worth starting with a ball of garlic and olive oil." This is the basic culinary conviction of the meritorious French-Italian firehouse cook Dick Marracq. His Nutmeg Veal Sauté and Herb Bordered Italian Roast (page 52) prove the wisdom of that maxim.

Boneless veal cutlet is the luxurious cut to get for this sauté. To suit the firehouse budget, Dick Marracq usually gets a rolled boneless shoulder veal roast, and slices it himself. His choice accompaniment to veal sauté is buttered bow-tie pasta.

NUTMEG VEAL SAUTÉ

1 pound boneless veal sliced about ¼ inch thick
Flour seasoned with salt and pepper
2 tablespoons *each* olive oil and butter
1 medium-sized onion, finely chopped
1 small clove garlic, minced or mashed
¼ cup finely chopped fresh parsley
1 cup beef broth
½ cup dry white table wine
½ can (6-ounce size) tomato paste
½ teaspoon ground nutmeg

Dip each veal piece in seasoned flour, and brown in olive oil and butter heated together in a large frying pan. Set browned veal aside. Add onions to drippings remaining in frying pan, and sauté until limp; add garlic and parsley and sauté until coated with oil. Stir into onion mixture the broth, wine, and tomato paste; cook for a few minutes, stirring, to blend. Return browned veal to frying pan, covering it with sauce. Sprinkle nutmeg over top. Bake in a moderate oven (350°), uncovered, for 45 minutes or until veal is very tender. (If necessary, add a little hot water to liquid in pan.) Makes 3 to 4 servings.

Dick Marracq, Engine Company No. 34

The cook's caution: "Use just the least little bit of thyme."

CHEESE-CRISPED VEAL CHOPS

4 large veal rib chops, cut 1 inch thick
Salt and pepper
Flour
1 small onion, minced
¼ cup grated or shredded Parmesan or mixed Parmesan and Romano cheeses
Crumbled dried thyme
Salad oil

Season chops generously with salt and pepper. Dust with flour. Press onions into chop surfaces, and gently pound in with plate edge or handle of a wooden spoon. Sprinkle chops on both sides with cheese and a small pinch of thyme, and pound in. Heat a generous amount of salad oil in a frying pan, add chops, and quickly brown on both sides. Pour off any excess oil. Cover chops and bake in a moderate oven (350°) for 20 minutes. Remove cover and bake 10 minutes more. Makes 4 servings.

John Bogue, Sr., Engine Company No. 17

Jim Rossbach is of Irish and German descent, but his Italian wife taught him how to make Veal Scaloppine, and from that he devised this. By careful cutting and trimming of the meat, he makes a tender-meated sauté out of economical veal stew meat. Serve it over hot rice, first browned in butter and oil, then steamed.

ITALIAN VEAL IN WINE

1½ pounds veal stew meat
Flour
About 3 tablespoons *each* butter and
  salad oil
Salt and pepper
1 large onion, finely chopped
1 cup dry white wine
1 clove garlic, minced or mashed
¼ teaspoon *each* crumbled dried rosemary and oregano
½ pound fresh mushrooms, thinly
  sliced
1 can (about 8 ounces) pitted black
  olives, drained
Hot cooked rice

Slicing across the grain (to cut fibers short), cut veal into small pieces (about 1-inch cubes); remove all gristle. Dust with flour. Brown veal on all sides over medium heat in about 2 tablespoons *each* of the butter and salad oil heated in a frying pan. Remove browned meat to a heavy kettle with cover; season with salt and pepper. Meantime, in a separate pan, sauté onions just until golden in 1 tablespoon *each* butter and salad oil. Add onions to veal along with wine, garlic, rosemary, and oregano. Cover and simmer slowly for 30 minutes, gently turning occasionally. Add mushrooms, cover, and continue simmering for 30 minutes more. Add olives and just heat through. Correct seasoning with salt and pepper. Serve over rice. Makes 4 to 6 servings.

Jim Rossbach, Engine Company No. 38

This is rich.

VEAL PARMIGIANA

4 servings boneless veal steak sliced ¼
  inch thick
Salt and pepper
Flour
1 egg
1 tablespoon water
Fine dry bread crumbs
Equal parts olive oil and butter
1 can (8 ounces) tomato sauce
¼ teaspoon crumbled dried oregano
½ pound Mozzarella cheese, thinly
  sliced
½ cup grated Parmesan cheese
Paprika

Season veal with salt and pepper; dust with flour and shake off excess. Beat egg with water. Dip meat into egg mixture, then into bread crumbs. Place in a single layer on a platter and chill in refrigerator for 1½ to 2 hours. Quickly brown veal (about 1 to 2 minutes each side) in a generous amount of hot melted butter and oil in a frying pan. Place browned meat in a single layer in a greased shallow baking pan. Meantime, combine tomato sauce and oregano, heat to boiling, and simmer a few minutes. Arrange Mozzarella cheese over meat to almost cover each piece. Spoon seasoned tomato sauce over meat. Sprinkle with Parmesan cheese. Spoon frying pan drippings over meat (about 1 teaspoon drippings for each piece of meat). Sprinkle lightly with paprika. Bake in a slow oven (325°) for 22 minutes (or until Parmesan browns slightly). Makes 4 servings.

Ray Hines, Engine Company No. 8

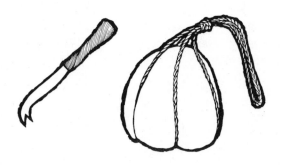

John Hearne invented these elegant little nuggets of sausage and veal, and, with justified authority, warns, "These are no good unless they're over rice; they're made for the rice."

You must use fine-quality lean pork sausages for this; and prepare them as directed—so the sausage will be firm within the veal. It's a good idea to prepare the sausages the night before.

VEAL AND SAUSAGE BROCHETTE

¾ pound fine-quality link pork
   sausages
Water
2 pounds veal for scaloppine (boneless
   veal cutlet, pounded very thin)
½ cup flour, seasoned with ½ teaspoon salt and ¼ teaspoon pepper
Olive oil
1 bunch green onions (white part only),
   thinly sliced
3 stalks celery, finely chopped
½ cup chopped fresh parsley
4 small cloves garlic, minced or mashed
½ teaspoon commercially packaged
   mixed Italian dry herbs
⅛ teaspoon *each* celery salt and
   coarsely ground black pepper
¼ cup olive oil
2 cups dry white wine
1 pound fresh mushrooms, thickly
   sliced
1 cup sour cream
1 tablespoon chopped chives
Salt and pepper
Hot steamed white rice

Cover sausages with cold water, slowly bring just to boiling point, remove from heat, let cool in water, drain, chill thoroughly; cut each sausage into thirds or about 1¼-inch pieces. Cut veal into strips as wide as sausage pieces, and wrap each veal strip around a sausage piece; secure with a toothpick. Shake veal rolls in seasoned flour in a clean paper bag. In a large frying pan, brown veal rolls well on all sides in olive oil. Transfer rolls to a clean kettle (about 3-quart size) with cover. Sprinkle rolls with onions, celery, parsley, garlic, mixed Italian herbs, celery salt, and pepper. Add ¼ cup olive oil and the wine. Cover tightly and simmer *very slowly* for 1 hour. Stir in sliced mushrooms, cover, and simmer slowly for 30 minutes more. Just before serving, stir in sour cream and chives; taste and correct seasoning; heat through. Serve over rice. Makes 6 servings.

John Hearne, Engine Company No. 9

North Italian San Franciscans eat a lot of veal. And a stuffed veal pocket (cima) is a good cook's specialty in many a household. Almost all stuffing mixtures are basically of spinach or Swiss chard and eggs. But from there on, the stuffing is up to the fancy of the cook. Additions might be Italian sausages, cheeses, bread crumbs, onions, parsley, mushrooms, nutmeg, oregano, marjoram, rosemary, pine nuts . . .

Cima is also a specialty of several Italian firehouse cooks—and they blend a stuffing to suit their whims.

Al Boccone makes cima as his father did—with chard, and Italian sausages, and a Marsala glaze to finish. You can substitute bits of leftover chicken or turkey for the sausage in the stuffing—or use a little of both. In any case, you'll have to taste and sniff the stuffing and add salt, pepper, and herbs according to the spiciness of the sausages or poultry you use. It's important to keep the veal skin moist with basting throughout roasting, so it will cut easily and cleanly at carving time. If you wish, add a few sliced green onions and some chopped parsley to the pan drippings during the last 10 minutes of roasting to make richly seasoned drippings for gravy making.

If you make too much stuffing for the veal pocket (as Pop Boccone did intentionally), you get an extra bonus of Piccola Frittatas: Spoon the stuffing mixture into a little heated oil in a frying pan and brown on both sides to make little patties. Serve hot as a vegetable side dish (excellent with roast chicken). Or let cool and tuck into a crusty roll for a sandwich. (The following recipe makes enough extra stuffing for a few Piccola Frittatas.)

THE BOCCONE CIMA

1 veal breast (about 3 pounds) with pocket for stuffing
Salt and pepper
2 finely chopped green onions with part of the green tops
1 clove garlic, minced or mashed
¼ cup finely chopped fresh parsley
Olive oil
3 bunches Swiss chard, trimmed, cooked just until tender, drained and squeezed dry, and finely chopped
4 eggs, slightly beaten
½ pound Italian garlic link sausages cut from casings, crumbled, browned, and drained
¾ cup grated Parmesan cheese
About ¼ teaspoon crumbled dried marjoram
About ⅛ teaspoon crumbled dried rosemary

Hot water
About ¼ cup Marsala

Sprinkle veal surfaces with salt and pepper. Sauté green onions, garlic, and parsley in a small amount of olive oil until limp. Mix together thoroughly with remaining ingredients except water and Marsala to make stuffing. Spoon stuffing lightly into veal pocket; close with small skewers or sew shut. Place in a shallow roasting pan, bone side down, and rub veal surface with olive oil. Bake in a slow oven (300°) for 2¼ hours. (Baste frequently with water; during last 30 minutes of roasting, baste with water and Marsala.) Allow to stand 20 to 30 minutes. Carve into slices. Makes about 6 servings.

Al Boccone, Engine Company No. 9

Known as "The Frenchman," Rene Codis is dapper, sharp, with twinkling kind eyes, and an imaginative way with food.

Inspired by the traits of cima, he dreamed up another marvelous meat compound: A pork roast stuffed with sweet Italian sausages (pork spiced with white wine, anise, sugar, garlic, etc.). He handles it as a regular pork roast—potatoes browned with it, applesauce served with it.

Two requirements to recreate it: (1) a source of sweet spiced Italian pork sausages; (2) a meatman who likes to experiment and to carry out special customer wishes.

A REMARKABLE ROAST

Ask your meatman to bone a loin of pork, replace the bone with Italian anise sausages in casings, roll, and tie. Roast as a regular pork roast. (Roast a 3-pound roast for 2½ hours in a slow oven [325°].) Allow to stand for about 15 minutes before carving. Makes 6 servings.

Rene Codis, Engine Company No. 40

The sauce is mellow with spices and Sherry.

SHERRY-MACE SAUCE FOR HAM

½ cup *each* water and raisins
¼ cup vinegar
1½ teaspoons grated orange peel
2 tablespoons orange juice
½ cup brown sugar, firmly packed
2 tablespoons cornstarch
½ teaspoon salt
¼ teaspoon ground mace
⅛ teaspoon *each* ground cinnamon
   and cloves
⅔ cup dry Sherry

Combine water, raisins, vinegar, orange peel and orange juice in a saucepan, and simmer for 5 minutes or until raisins are plump and tender. Combine thoroughly the brown sugar, cornstarch, salt, mace, cinnamon, and cloves, and stir into raisin mixture. Cook over medium heat, stirring, until thickened and clear. Add Sherry, and continue cooking, stirring, until well blended, about 5 minutes. Makes about 1¼ cups or sauce for 6 servings of ham.

Lieutenant Al Kilkeary,
Truck Company No. 13

Ted Dal Broi stuffs double-thick pork chops fat and full with herb-seasoned spinach, then bakes them to a glowing deep brown.

SPINACH-STUFFED PORK CHOPS

6 large double-thick pork chops (loin or rib), cut 1½ inches thick and with a pocket for stuffing
Salt and pepper
1 package (12 ounces) frozen chopped spinach, cooked and well-drained
1 teaspoon lemon juice
¼ cup cracker meal
⅜ teaspoon salt
⅛ teaspoon crumbled dried oregano
1/16 teaspoon black pepper

Season pork chops generously on outside and inside pocket with salt and pepper. Combine spinach, lemon juice, cracker meal, the ⅜ teaspoon salt, oregano, and the 1/16 teaspoon pepper and spoon into pork-chop pockets. Arrange meat in a single layer in baking pan, and bake in a moderate oven (350°) for 40 minutes. Turn over and bake 35 minutes more. Makes 4 servings.

Ted Dal Broi, Truck Company No. 5

"Everybody likes 'em" . . . Bob Rose

BROWN-SUGARED LEMON PORK CHOPS

6 double-thick loin pork chops (1 to 1½ inches thick)
Salt and pepper
2 eggs
2 tablespoons milk
Cracker meal
Shortening
About 2 tablespoons brown sugar
Worcestershire sauce
3 lemons, thinly sliced
2 cans (8 ounces *each*) tomato sauce

Season chops on both sides with salt and pepper. Beat eggs and milk together. Dip chops into egg batter, then into cracker meal to coat. Brown chops on both sides in a small amount of heated shortening in a frying pan; place in a single layer in a large shallow baking pan. Top each chop with about a teaspoon of brown sugar, a few drops of Worcestershire, and several overlapping lemon slices. Pour tomato sauce over chops. Bake in a moderate oven (350°) for 45 minutes or until tender. Makes 6 servings.

Bob Rose, Engine Company No. 21

The thick spareribs from the shoulder end of the pork loin split lengthwise make meatier servings than the usual rack of spareribs. Ask your meatman to separate them into choplike pieces, cutting between ribs.

SWEET AND SOUR SPARERIBS, COUNTRY STYLE

1 side country-style spareribs (about 3 pounds), cut into rib pieces
Salt and pepper
2 medium-sized onions
1 green pepper, quartered lengthwise and each quarter cut into thirds
2 tablespoons salad oil
1 can (about 14 ounces) pineapple chunks
2 teaspoons cornstarch
3 tablespoons vinegar
½ teaspoon ground ginger

Season spareribs generously with salt and pepper. Place in a single layer in a shallow baking pan and bake in a hot oven (425°) for 20 minutes. Meantime, cut onions, top to bottom, into quarters and separate leaves. Sauté onions and peppers in oil just until limp. Drain syrup from pineapple into a saucepan. Stir together a little of the syrup with cornstarch to make a smooth paste, and pour into syrup in saucepan. Cook, stirring, until thickened and clear. Stir in vinegar and ginger. Combine browned meat, sautéed peppers and onions, pineapple chunks, and sauce. Cover and bake in a moderate oven (350°) for 45 minutes. Gently stir once or twice. Makes 4 to 6 servings.

Bob Burns, Truck Company No. 3

Jack Keating ties together uniform pork chops and bakes them as a pork loin roast—but with onions tucked between chops and paprika over the tops. At serving time, he simply cuts the strings, and the roast is carved, ready to serve.

Make a brown gravy from the roast drippings if you wish.

PAPRIKA PORK

6 center-cut loin pork chops, cut ¾ inch thick
Salt, pepper, and paprika
1 large onion, thinly sliced

Season chops on both sides with salt, pepper, and paprika. Place chops together to resemble a loin roast, tucking several onion slices between chops; tie together with string. Place on rack in roasting pan, fat side up. Sprinkle top generously with paprika. Roast in a slow oven (325°) for 2 hours. Cut string and separate chops; serve onion slices with each. Makes 6 servings.

Jack Keating, Engine Company No. 3

CHAPTER 6

when the bell goes off

FIRE

A FALSE ALARM
AY COST A LIFE

BREAK

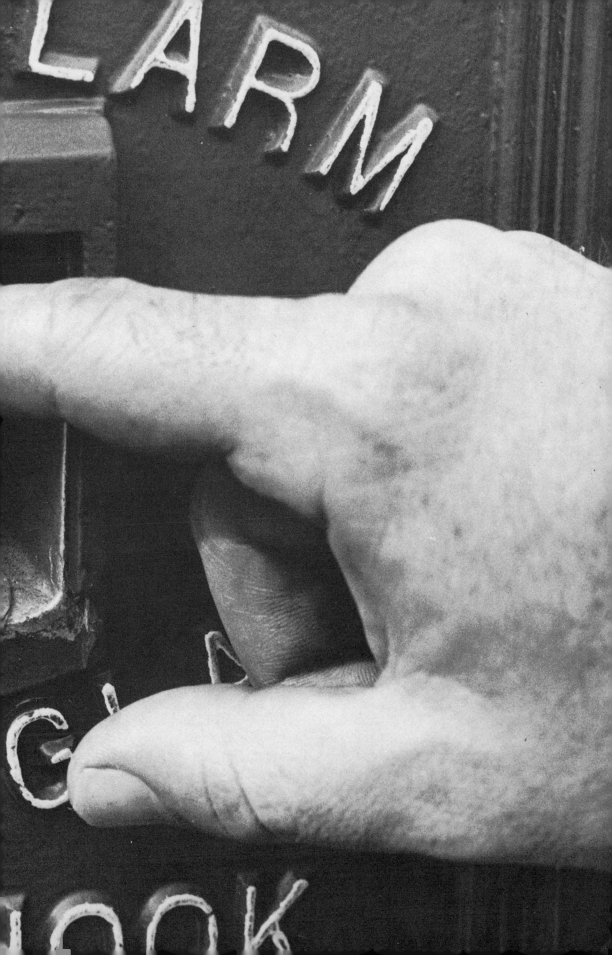

A PASSING MOTORIST has seen wisps of smoke curling from an upper-story apartment window and turned in an alarm at the box on the corner. Inside an engine company a fireman has counted the taps of the bell and shouted "It's inside!", and the firemen, luxuriously sprinkling fresh Parmesan onto platters heaped full of fragrant spaghetti, drop everything. They know the fire is inside their area. Within seconds the watchman has double-checked the signal he has heard with the data on his register tape and the officer has checked the proper assignment card to see which companies are due and which are available. They're first due, and away they roar from quarters. From "spotting the hydrant" to the intricate two-man operation of connecting pumper to hydrant to the officer's "size-up" and decision as to mode of operations, all movements are swift and sure.

NOW THE ONLY SPAGHETTI the firemen are concerned with is the

"spaghetti" snaking through the streets—the pressure-swollen lines of hose charged with water. The street alarm has brought to the scene three engines, two ladder trucks, a Chief's "buggy," a rescue squad, and a salvage company. Perhaps the fire proves to be a "worker"—and the battalion chief must radio to Central Fire Alarm Headquarters for a greater alarm.

EVEN AFTER THE BLAZE has been extinguished, activity doesn't stop. If there are children standing by, the battalion chief may speak a few words of warning to them of the danger of playing with matches. The origin of the fire is determined, and if suspicious, the Bureau of Fire Investigation steps in. The conditions which prevailed at the fire may be simulated in the next day's training session at the Fire College. Meanwhile, back at the firehouse, the cold spaghetti stands ready and waiting for the weary fire fighters to return.

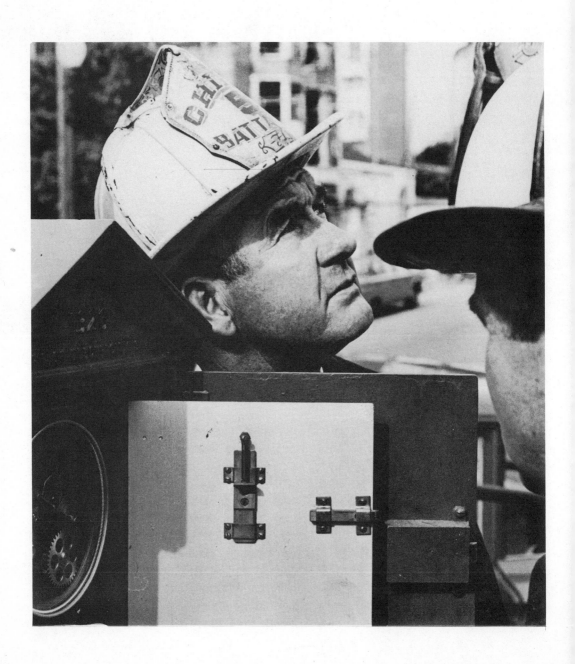

CHAPTER 7

seafood and poultry

SEAFOOD AND POULTRY

Friday's cook begins with one thing certain: it's got to be fish. But the prospect holds no peril because Fisherman's Wharf, the fresh fish markets of Chinatown, and the waters off San Francisco yield up such succulent and tempting morsels from the sea.

Occasionally, when all the firemen in a house are in an expansive mood, there's the luxury of cioppino—nutty Pacific crab so fresh it's alive when it goes into the pot, layers of clams, prawns, white fish—all steaming in a fragrant, invigorating Italian fisherman's sauce of tomatoes, garlic, white wine, herbs.

Poultry in the firehouse pot promises fine eating, easily financed.

The tomato sauce should be thick; the crab adds its own juices to thin it down.

CRAB CIOPPINO TREGANZA

2 large onions, chopped
5 stalks celery, very thinly sliced
4 medium-sized carrots, very thinly
   sliced
1 cup chopped fresh parsley
About 6 tablespoons olive oil
1 large clove garlic, minced or mashed
5 cans (8 ounces *each*) tomato sauce
2 cups water
⅛ teaspoon *each* crumbled dried
   thyme, rosemary, and sage
3 live crabs, washed and cracked
3 pounds cockles (or clams) in shells,
   well scrubbed
1 pound medium-sized raw prawns
About 2 pounds fillet of cod (or other
   white fish)
⅓ cup dry white wine
Salt and pepper
Additional chopped fresh parsley

In a large kettle, sauté onions, celery, carrots, and parsley in olive oil until onions are limp. Add garlic, tomato sauce, water, thyme, rosemary, and sage; cover and simmer for about 45 minutes or until carrots and celery are tender. Add crab; top with cockles. Cover and simmer 30 minutes. Add prawns; top with cod. Cover and simmer 10 minutes more. (Do not stir, but gently shake pot occasionally.) Add wine, season sauce with salt and pepper if necessary, and simmer 5 minutes more. Ladle into large serving bowls. Sprinkle with parsley. Makes 6 generous servings.

Art Treganza,
Airport Rescue Company No. 3

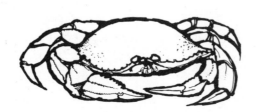

Retired Jimmy Higgins is well remembered as "one of the best" of all cooks. On Friday nights, he'd do a fish fry—with sole. His trick was to soak the sole fillets in salt water, to freshen them and firm them for frying. He'd serve them with fresh lemon slices and tartar sauce.

CRISP CRUSTED SOLE

4 sole fillets
Cold salted water
Beaten eggs
Cornflake crumbs
Salt
Lemon slices and tartar sauce

Place sole fillets in salt water for 5 minutes. Drain well. Dip into beaten egg, then into crumbs; pat crumbs into fish.

Place on a platter and allow to stand for a few minutes until crumb coating sets. Heat equal parts salad oil and butter ¼ inch deep in a frying pan. Add sole and brown quickly on one side; turn over, sprinkle with salt, and brown quickly on second side. Serve immediately with lemon slices and tartar sauce. Makes 4 servings.

Jimmy Higgins,
Retired from Engine Company No. 41

TARRAGON TARTAR SAUCE

½ cup mayonnaise
1 cup chopped dill pickle
3 tablespoons grated onion
2 tablespoons finely chopped fresh
   parsley
1 tablespoon fresh lemon juice
½ teaspoon *each* crumbled dried tarragon, seafood seasoning, and finely chopped capers
⅛ teaspoon salt
$\frac{1}{16}$ teaspoon pepper

Combine all ingredients thoroughly. Cover and chill 2 hours. Makes about 1½ cups.

Noble Sonne, Engine Company No. 9

Cliff Kahn steals his mom's recipes:

SOLE À LA SHERRY

4 sole fillets (about 1 pound)
1 package (1¾ ounces) dry mushroom soup mix
1 cup sour cream
3 tablespoons dry Sherry
1 tablespoon lemon juice
¼ teaspoon crumbled sweet basil
3 tablespoons butter

Mix together in a saucepan the mushroom soup, sour cream, Sherry, lemon
juice, and sweet basil. Cook over very
low heat, stirring, until heated through.
Melt butter in a large frying pan (or
other large shallow pan). Arrange sole
in a single layer in pan. Pour mushroom sauce over top. Cover and cook
over medium heat for 7 minutes or
until fish flakes easily with a fork.
Makes 3 to 4 servings.

Cliff Kahn, Engine Company No. 14

OYSTERS IN THE OVEN

2 pints medium-sized fresh oysters
½ cup *each* cracker meal and flour
1½ teaspoons salt
¾ teaspoon crumbled dried sweet basil
½ teaspoon pepper
¼ teaspoon onion powder
½ cup *each* butter and salad oil
Fresh lemon slices

Roll oysters in mixture of cracker meal,
flour, salt, basil, pepper, and onion
powder to coat thoroughly. Combine
butter and oil in a shallow baking pan
(about 9 by 13 inches) and heat in a
moderate oven (375°) until bubbling.
Add oysters and bake for 20 minutes;
turn and bake 20 minutes more or
until golden brown. Serve with lemon
slices. Makes 6 servings.

Herb Muzio, Engine Company No. 44

Jim King's deep-frying batter becomes a light, delicate crusting ("just like cake") around whatever it coats. Try it on prawns or small pieces of cooked chicken or veal.

Dry chilling the bowl seems to be important; so does ice-cold water.

SCALLOP FRY

1¼ cups flour
1 teaspoon baking powder
½ teaspoon *each* salt and sugar
1 cup ice water
1 egg, beaten
2 pounds scallops
Oil for deep frying
Lemon wedges

Thoroughly chill mixing bowl. Sift together flour, baking powder, salt, and sugar into chilled bowl. Add water gradually, stirring to mix thoroughly. Add egg, and beat mixture with a wire whisk until smooth. Dip scallops into batter. Place in heated oil (350° to 375°) for deep frying and cook until golden. Drain for a moment on paper towels. Serve with lemon. Makes 6 servings.

Jim King, Engine Company No. 2

Even if you use canned crab, it must be Pacific coast crab (Dungeness).

CRAB À LA JIM KING

½ cup butter
½ cup flour
1 teaspoon salt
4 cups milk
1½ teaspoons Worcestershire sauce
2 cans (2¼ ounces *each*) sliced ripe
 olives, drained
1 can (4 ounces) pimentos, drained
 and diced
1 pound (about 2 cups) flaked Pacific
 crab meat (or 2 cans [about 7 ounces
 each] Dungeness crab, drained)
Hot buttered steamed rice sprinkled
 with paprika

In a saucepan, melt butter, and stir in flour and salt to make a smooth paste. Gradually add milk, cooking and stirring, until sauce is smooth and thickened. Stir in Worcestershire. Fold in olives, pimentos, and crab, and heat through. Serve over rice. Makes 6 servings.

Jim King, Engine Company No. 2

His colleagues say Art Treganza is "without a doubt, the best cook in the Fire Department." They say his Chicken Fricassee is part of their proof.

CHICKEN FRICASSEE WITH FRESH TAGLIARINI

1 stewing hen (about 4 pounds), cut into pieces (include heart and gizzard)
Shortening
Salt and pepper
1 large onion, chopped
¼ cup chopped fresh parsley
1 clove garlic, minced or mashed
¼ teaspoon crumbled dried rosemary
2 cans (8 ounces *each*) tomato sauce
1 small can (1 pound) peeled whole tomatoes
1 cup water
About ½ ounce dried mushrooms, soaked, squeezed dry, and chopped
Tagliarini (Recipe below. Or prepare ¾ pound dry tagliarini according to package directions)
¼ cup grated Parmesan cheese

In a large frying pan or kettle with cover, brown chicken pieces thoroughly. Remove any shortening in excess of ¼ cup. Season chicken with salt and pepper. Add onion and sauté, gently stirring, until tender and golden. Add parsley, garlic, and rosemary, and sauté until coated with oil. Add tomato sauce, tomatoes, and water. Cover and simmer for 2 hours; stir occasionally. Season sauce with salt and pepper to taste. Add mushrooms, cover, and cook chicken 1 hour more or until very tender. Serve chicken pieces alongside tagliarini. Ladle chicken sauce over tagliarini and sprinkle with cheese. Makes 6 servings.

TAGLIARINI

Separate strands of 1 pound fresh tagliarini and spread on baking sheet or other clean surface for 1 hour before cooking. Cook tagliarini for 10 minutes in boiling salted water with 2 tablespoons olive oil added. Rinse and drain well.

Art Treganza,
Airport Rescue Company No. 3

"I just think of things I think would taste good together." (That's how Jack Kermoian created this chicken dish—and why it has no name.)

The sequence of salt-pepper-paprika-browning seems to be important.

KERMOIAN'S CHICKEN

1 clove garlic, cut in half
⅓ cup olive oil
1 frying chicken, 2½ to 3 pounds, cut into serving pieces
Salt and pepper
Paprika
1 medium-sized onion, cut in half crosswise, then thinly sliced from top to bottom
½ pound fresh mushrooms, sliced
4 green onions with 3 inches of the green tops, cut in half lengthwise, then cut diagonally into 1-inch slices
1½ stalks celery, thinly sliced
1 can (2¼ ounces) sliced black olives, drained
¼ cup dry Sherry

Sauté garlic in olive oil in a large frying pan until lightly browned; discard garlic. Sprinkle chicken pieces on one side with salt, pepper, and paprika; place in frying pan, seasoned side down, and brown well. Season second side of chicken pieces with salt, pepper, and paprika and turn chicken over. Sprinkle with sliced onion and mushrooms. Brown chicken well on second side, allowing onions to sauté until limp and golden. Add green onions, celery, and olives. Cook for just a few minutes. Pour Sherry over chicken. Bake in a moderate oven (350°) for 15 minutes. Makes 4 servings.

Jack Kermoian, Engine Company No. 15

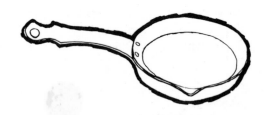

At Engine No. 3, A-shift firemen praise Johnny Charcho's version of Chicken and Rice: "best ever eaten."

The rice must cook in a well-seasoned chicken stock. Cook Charcho makes his own, simmering chicken giblets and necks for 2½ to 3 hours with seasonings of salt, oregano, mixed Italian herbs, onion, bell pepper, and celery tops.

PARMESAN CHICKEN AND RICE

3 frying chickens, 2 to 2½ pounds *each*, halved
1 can (10½ ounces) cream of mushroom soup
1 cup milk
1 package (about 1½ ounces) onion soup mix
Black pepper
Garlic powder
About 1 cup grated Parmesan cheese
Paprika
1½ cups long grain white rice cooked in well-seasoned chicken stock just until tender

Arrange chicken halves, bone side down, in a single layer in a large shallow baking pan. Combine mushroom soup, milk, and onion soup mix, and pour over chicken. Sprinkle with pepper and lightly with garlic powder. Bake in a moderate oven (350°) for 1 hour or until chicken is tender; baste occasionally. Sprinkle chicken with Parmesan cheese (about ½ cup) and paprika, and bake 10 minutes more. Remove chicken and sauce to warm serving platter; keep warm. Add rice to chicken baking pan, and stir to mix thoroughly with pan drippings. Sprinkle with Parmesan cheese and bake in a moderate oven (350°) for 10 to 15 minutes. Serve chicken and rice together. Makes 6 generous servings.

Johnny Charcho, Engine Company No. 3

A few hints from the chef: Use only brewed Japanese soy sauce. If you can get it, use Hawaiian sake for the wine ingredient. Do the 24-hour marinating if you think of it in time; if you don't, don't worry; the chicken will still be fine.

CHICKEN TERIYAKI

2 frying chickens, 2½ to 3 pounds, cut into serving pieces
2 cups brown sugar, firmly packed
1 cup dry white wine or Hawaiian sake
⅔ cup brewed Japanese soy sauce
3 to 4 cloves garlic, minced or mashed
¾ pound fresh mushrooms, thinly sliced
Steamed white rice

Place chicken pieces in deep glass or enamel bowl. Combine brown sugar, wine, soy, and garlic, and pour over chicken. Cover and allow to marinate in refrigerator for 24 hours. Arrange chicken pieces in single layer in shallow baking pan. Place mushrooms in marinade. Baste chicken with just enough marinade so bottom of baking pan is covered with liquid. Bake in a moderate oven (350°) for 1 hour or until glazed and tender. (Baste frequently throughout baking, adding just enough marinade to keep liquid in bottom of pan. After about 35 minutes' baking, turn chicken pieces, spread marinated mushrooms over them, and continue baking.) When chicken is done, remove to serving platter and keep warm. Combine in a saucepan any remaining marinade and the baking pan juices and mushrooms; quickly bring to a boil and serve as sauce over chicken and rice. Makes 6 servings.

Dick Paganelli, Engine Company No. 17

Andy Bronzovich's Slavonian ancestry doesn't preclude his virtuosity with Italian cuisine. Here he proves his mastery of cacciatore and pasta, and further insists that you must have Italian (or French) bread with this dinner.

The rich tomato sauce seasons the chicken, then sauces the pasta.

CHICKEN CACCIATORE WITH VERMICELLI

2 broiler chickens (about 2 pounds *each*), split in half
Flour seasoned with salt, pepper, and mixed Italian dry herbs
Olive oil
Tomato sauce
½ pound vermicelli, cooked just until tender and drained
Grated Parmesan cheese

Shake chicken halves in a clean paper bag filled with seasoned flour. In a large frying pan, brown chicken on both sides in a generous amount of heated olive oil. Arrange chicken in a single layer in a large baking pan; pour tomato sauce over. Bake, uncovered, in a slow oven (325°) for 1 hour or until chicken is tender. (After 45 minutes' baking, spoon half the sauce out of pan with chicken and combine it with cooked hot vermicelli. Keep warm in oven.) At serving time, arrange chicken on one serving platter, vermicelli on another. Sprinkle vermicelli liberally with Parmesan. Makes 4 generous servings.

TOMATO SAUCE

Sauté 2 medium-sized onions, chopped, and 1½ stalks celery, chopped, in 6 tablespoons olive oil until limp. Add 1 clove garlic, minced or mashed; ½ pound fresh mushrooms, sliced; and ¼ cup chopped fresh parsley; sauté, stirring, until mushrooms are tender. Add 1 can (14½ ounces) solid-pack tomatoes; 1 can (8 ounces) tomato sauce; ½ can (6-ounce size) tomato paste; ½ teaspoon salt; ¼ teaspoon mixed Italian dry herbs, and ⅛ teaspoon freshly ground black pepper. Cover and simmer for 1½ hours, stirring occasionally. Add ½ cup dry white wine, cover and simmer for 30 minutes more.

Andy Bronzovich, Truck Company No. 3

This was Captain Locke's father's recipe; now it's a firehouse classic.

SWEET POTATO-APPLE STUFFING FOR TURKEY

Turkey heart, liver, and gizzard, cooked until tender

2 loaves of 2-to-4-day-old bread

1 large unpeeled apple, cored and sliced

1 uncooked sweet potato, peeled and sliced

2 medium-sized onions, peeled and sliced

6 to 8 stalks celery

1 cup chopped fresh parsley

1 cup melted butter

Salt (about 2 teaspoons)

Poultry seasoning (about 1½ teaspoons)

Ground sage (about 1 teaspoon)

Pepper (about 1 teaspoon)

Broth from cooking giblets

Put turkey giblets, bread, apple, sweet potato, onions, and celery through meat grinder fitted with a medium blade. Mix thoroughly with parsley, butter, seasonings to taste, and enough broth to moisten. Makes stuffing for a 12-pound bird.

Captain Arthur Locke,
Engine Company No. 37

CHAPTER 8

barbecue specialties

BARBECUE SPECIALTIES

Almost every firehouse manages to finance some sort of barbecue brazier. Barbecue fires, of course, are well tended.

You can apply this Armenian barbecuing treatment to any steak for barbecuing or broiling. But Armenian specialist Jack Kermoian recommends chuck—for flavor and for this unique butterflying treatment. The results are a wonderfully juicy steak, rich with beef flavor—and subtly winey.

You ask your meatman for a boneless center-cut chuck steak, butterflied to make an inch-thick steak. Or if you're skilled at meat manipulation, prepare the steak yourself: buy a center-cut chuck roast 2 inches thick; remove bone from meat and trim away fat and gristle, keeping meat in one piece; slice in half crosswise, cutting to, but not through, one side of roast; fold open to make a very large steak 1 inch thick.

BARBECUED BUTTERFLIED CHUCK STEAK

Boneless center-cut chuck steak, butterflied to an inch-thick steak
Salt, freshly ground black pepper, and paprika
1 large onion, thinly sliced from top to bottom
About ¾ cup dry red table wine

Season steak on both sides with salt, pepper, and paprika. Place steak and onions in a large bowl or enamel pan and pour over enough wine to almost cover; cover, chill, and marinate overnight. Remove meat from marinade and grill over hot charcoal to doneness you desire. Meantime, heat the marinating onions in wine; serve onions alongside steak. Makes 3 to 4 servings.

Jack Kermoian, Engine Company No. 15

Not everyone knows about the flatiron roast. But old-time butchers do. And firemen who are savvy about beef cuts do. It's the iron-shaped (triangular) piece of meat running through the blade, alongside the Jewish fillet. (In your part of the country this cut may be known as a triangular pot roast or shoulder lift.) When filleted, it's sometimes termed plank steak. The whole roast weighs about 2 pounds, it's nicely marbled, and it barbecue-broils beautifully.

To barbecue it Ed Limberg's way, and turn out juicy, rare, wonderful steaks:

PLANK STEAK BARBECUE

Ask your meatman for a flatiron roast; have him trim it and remove center gristle, and fillet it into 2 steaks. Rub steak surfaces with a crushed clove of garlic; season with salt and pepper. Place on grill very close (within 1 inch) to hot charcoal for about ½ to 1 minute to sear; raise to 3 inches above charcoal and cook for 4 to 5 minutes more. Turn steaks, and broil second side like the first side, first searing, then grilling above coals. Serves 2 firemen or 4 usual eaters.

Ed Limberg, Engine Company No. 21

 Fat garlic sausages bristle and brown over charcoal under a melting saucing of Swiss cheese. Pass mustard, and tuck hot sausages into rye-with-caraway buns.

SWISS SAUCED
BARBECUE SAUSAGE

Split plump garlic frankfurters in half, lengthwise, and fold open. Place, cut side down, on barbecue grill over medium coals. Grill until bubbling and hot. Turn, top each with a thin slice of natural Swiss cheese, and grill on second side until sausage is browned and cheese begins to melt.

John E. Putman, Truck Company No. 3

"Nobody'll ever believe they can eat it when they see you doing it," warns the creator. He sprinkles a barbecued chuck roast with a fearful amount of dry mustard and Worcestershire, punctures it ferociously with two forks, then carves the meat into tender slices and serves it with mustard-mingled juices spooned over the top.

MUSTARD-BARBECUED CHUCK ROAST

2-inch thick chuck roast (about 5 pounds)
Unseasoned meat tenderizer
1 clove garlic, peeled and slivered
2 tablespoons *each* dry mustard and Worcestershire sauce

Sprinkle meat generously on both sides with meat tenderizer; with a sharp knife, pierce roast in a few places, and insert slivers of garlic; allow to stand at room temperature for 1½ hours. Barbecue meat over medium-hot coals for 20 minutes on each side. Remove to carving platter. Sprinkle one side of meat with half the mustard and half the Worcestershire; with two forks, pierce through the meat over entire surface. Turn meat, sprinkle second side with remaining mustard and Worcestershire, and pierce as before. Carve roast into "little roasts," following the lines of bone, fat, and gristle; slice each little roast thinly, across the grain (as if it were a large roast). Spoon juices over meat slices. Makes 4 servings.

Lieutenant Frank Waldeyer,
Engine Company No. 10

The culinary wonders of San Francisco's Chinatown are bound to extend their influence to firehouse cooking. One Oriental delicacy is Chief Baumeister's sauce for barbecued spareribs. Chinese proprietors of the Dong and Kee Grocery gave him the recipe.

In San Francisco, the Hoisin Sauce ingredient calls for a shopping trip to Chinatown or a neighborhood Oriental grocery. In most metropolitan areas, you can find it in Oriental markets and specialty stores.

DONG AND KEE BARBECUED SPARERIBS

3 sides pork spareribs (about 6
   pounds), cut in half across the ribs
¼ cup catsup
3 tablespoons soy sauce
2 tablespoons Chinese Hoisin Sauce
4 teaspoons sugar
1 teaspoon salt
Dash of pepper
1 clove garlic, minced or mashed

Cut sparerib strips into 3-to-4-rib pieces. Combine catsup, soy, Hoisin, sugar, salt, pepper, and garlic, and brush over both sides of sparerib pieces. Allow to stand 3 to 4 hours. Grill slowly over low-glowing barbecue coals, turning frequently, for 40 minutes. (Watch carefully; spareribs should become golden, not charred.) Makes 6 servings.

Battalion Chief Fred Baumeister,
Battalion District No. 5

If you like your lamb slightly rare and vegetables well done but deep with flavor, the barbecue-grilling timing is right. (If that is not your choice, barbecue vegetables separately from lamb and time separately.)

Serve with Jack Kermoian's Armenian Pilaff (page 137).

SHERRY SHISH KEBAB

5-to-6-pound leg of lamb, boned, well trimmed with all gristle removed, and cut into 1-to-1½-inch cubes

Salt and freshly ground pepper

2 large white onions, thinly sliced from top to bottom

2 teaspoons paprika

About ¾ cup dry Sherry

16 small whole tomatoes

4 green peppers, cut in quarters, stem and seeds removed

16 small yellow onions, peeled

Season meat generously with salt and pepper. Place in a large bowl with onions; sprinkle with paprika. Add Sherry. Mix well. Place tomatoes, peppers, and onions on top of meat. Cover, chill, and marinate for 12 hours or overnight. Thread lamb cubes and vegetables on skewers. Barbecue over medium-hot charcoal, turning to cook on all sides until lamb is brown on the outside, slightly rare inside, about 20 minutes total. Makes 8 servings.

Jack Kermoian, Engine Company No. 15

The sour cream dipping sauce is optional, but recipe creator Frank Alianza says it makes it more Slavic.

LEMON SHASHLIK

5-to-6-pound leg of lamb, boned, well trimmed with all gristle removed, and cut into 2-to-2½-inch cubes
Salt and freshly ground black pepper
2 medium-sized white onions, sliced very thinly from top to bottom
2 lemons, cut into quarters
16 large whole fresh mushrooms
4 green peppers, quartered, stems and seeds removed
16 small whole onions
Sour cream

Sprinkle lamb generously with salt and very generously with pepper to season. Put into a bowl with onions. Squeeze juice of lemon quarters over meat, then add remaining lemon rind. Mix well and let stand at room temperature at least 4 hours; stir occasionally. Thread meat on skewers (or spit), alternating with mushrooms, peppers, and onions. Grill over medium-hot charcoal until done to your liking. Makes about 8 servings.

Frank Alianza, Engine Company No. 1

Whoever tries this sauce should do so knowing he's been given a hallowed recipe—original, long groomed, and long guarded. Only now, for a San Francisco fireman's book, does Jack Kermoian reveal the secret.

This recipe makes sauce for 2 to 3 frying chickens. Brush it on during just the last 10 or 15 minutes' grilling. (Jack Kermoian barbecues chicken pieces over medium-hot coals for a good 15 minutes each side, and if necessary, brushes them with a little olive oil during the grilling time before the sauce goes on. You needn't salt and pepper the chicken before grilling; the sauce does the total seasoning.)

JACK KERMOIAN'S SPECIAL BARBECUE SAUCE ESPECIALLY FOR CHICKEN

1 medium-sized onion, finely chopped
1 clove garlic, minced or mashed
½ cup salad oil
2 tablespoons brown sugar
1 tablespoon chili powder
2 teaspoons salt
1 teaspoon *each* dry mustard and
   paprika
1 large dash cayenne
Pinch *each* of crumbled dried thyme
   and marjoram
2 tablespoons water
2 cans (8 ounces *each*) tomato sauce
½ cup *each* fresh lemon juice and
   water
2 drops liquid smoke

Slowly sauté onion and garlic in salad oil until tender, but not brown. Mix brown sugar, chili powder, salt, mustard, paprika, cayenne, thyme, and marjoram to a paste with the 2 tablespoons water; stir into onion mixture. Add tomato sauce, lemon juice, ½ cup water, and liquid smoke. Boil gently, uncovered, stirring, for 10 to 15 minutes. Brush on chicken during last 10 minutes of barbecuing. Makes barbecuing sauce for 2 to 3 chickens.

Jack Kermoian, Engine Company No. 15

Plan on one thick, meaty lamb chop per serving. You trim away all the lamb fat so it won't char and make a sooty deposit on the meat.

BARBECUED GARLIC LAMB BLOCKS

Trim all excess fat from lamb blocks cut 1½ inches thick. Rub meat surfaces with cut cloves of garlic, salt, and freshly ground black pepper to season generously. Barbecue over medium-hot coals for about 10 minutes on each side or until done to your liking.

Rene Codis, Engine Company No. 40

CHAPTER 9

sport fish and seafood, game

SPORT FISH AND SEAFOOD, GAME

When a fireman is not a fireman on duty, he's likely to be a sportsman out hunting or fishing. Firemen are enthusiastic outdoorsmen; they have fishing cabins in the Russian River country, hunting cabins in the high Sierras; they work double and trade shifts to clear stretches of time for a trek out of doors.

The night a fisherman-fireman brings in a freshly caught salmon is the night for Bill Smith to take over, and make his sauce for fresh salmon steaks. Reading the recipe, you wouldn't think the sauce unusual. But taste it and you know that here is a proper balance of ingredients to complement fresh Pacific salmon. It's a mellow blend, without the usual sharpness of many Italian tomato sauces.

ONION-SMOTHERED SALMON STEAKS

3 medium-sized onions, chopped
1 green bell pepper, chopped
5 stalks celery, chopped
½ cup olive oil
½ cup chopped fresh parsley
2 cloves garlic, minced or mashed
2 cans (about 14 ounces *each*) tomato purée
2 cans (8 ounces *each*) tomato sauce
1 cup dry white wine
1 teaspoon salt
¼ teaspoon *each* pepper and mixed Italian dry herbs
8 to 10 salmon steaks, each 1 inch thick
Salt

In large frying pan or kettle, sauté onions, pepper, and celery in olive oil until limp. Stir in parsley and garlic, and sauté until coated with oil. Stir in tomato purée, tomato sauce, wine, salt, pepper, and Italian herbs. Cover loosely and simmer for 1 hour, stirring occasionally. Arrange salmon steaks in a single layer in a baking pan, salt lightly, pour sauce over, and bake for 30 minutes in a moderate oven (350°). Makes 8 to 10 servings.

Bill Smith, Chief's Operator

The simplest way is the best way with abalone steaks, according to Roy Perry:

SIZZLED ABALONE

"Dip abalone steaks in beaten eggs, then in cracker crumbs. Put them in very hot butter and oil in a frying pan. Count to ten and turn them over. Count to ten and take them out." Serve with fresh lemon.

Roy Perry, Chief's Operator,
Battalion District No. 2

Russ McKlem subscribes to the same way of cooking the abalone he gathers around Fort Ross and Jenner, *except* he "crumbs" the pounded steaks with wheat germ instead of cracker crumbs.

Russ McKlem, Engine Company No. 39

And John Bogue's abalone secret is just a little garlic in the egg batter: Rub a mixing bowl with a half clove of garlic; in bowl, beat eggs, and season them well with salt and pepper. Dip pounded abalone steaks into eggs, then into fine dry bread crumbs. Let abalone stand a few minutes, then dip again in bread crumbs. Fry fast (as above) in hot salad oil.

John Bogue, Sr., Engine Company No. 17

Striped bass is a great game fish in San Francisco Bay and off the California coast. But the good sport it offers doesn't outshine the good eating. If you don't have a fireman-fisherman to catch a striped bass for you and you don't catch one yourself, you can still apply this treatment to any whole fish of a similar size—or white fish fillets (and bake just until fish flakes with a fork). The fresh lemon and vegetable stuffing makes fresh fish taste even fresher.

STUFFED STRIPER

2 cans (8 ounces *each*) tomato sauce
2 teaspoons Worcestershire sauce
3 large onions, thinly sliced
2 green bell peppers, seeded and cut into thin strips
2 stalks celery, chopped
Whole striped bass (about 6 pounds), head removed
Salt
4 lemons, thinly sliced

Combine in a saucepan the tomato sauce, Worcestershire, and half of the onions, peppers, and celery; cook, stirring, for 10 to 15 minutes. Meantime, rub fish inside and out with salt, and stuff cavity with remaining onions, bell peppers, celery, and half the lemon slices; skewer or sew shut. Place fish in a greased shallow baking pan, and arrange remaining lemon slices over top. Pour tomato sauce over fish. Bake in a moderate oven (350°) for 40 minutes or until fish flakes easily with a fork. Makes about 8 servings.

Bob Rose, Engine Company No. 21

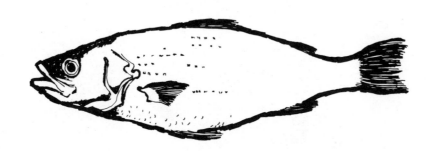

"Cockles and Rice was always a simple dish at home," recounts Art Treganza. "Then once I made it at the firehouse and the guys went nuts for it. After that, every time I went there—even when it wasn't Friday—they'd ask for Cockles and Rice."

Fireman Treganza does his clam-digging on the ocean side of Bolinas Bay. He tells how to check cockles (steaming clams) for loaded sand—and this is important: Before rinsing in fresh water, squeeze cockles together, two by two. If loaded with sand, a cockle will open; discard it. Also important is that you serve garlic bread with Cockles and Rice.

Adjust amounts of water and rice according to amount of broth you like.

COCKLES AND RICE

2 medium-sized onions, chopped
1 large clove garlic, minced or mashed
1 cup chopped fresh parsley
About 4 tablespoons olive oil
About 5 quarts water
2 or more cups long grain white rice
5 pounds cockles (clams) in shells,
    rinsed and scrubbed
Salt and freshly ground black pepper
Additional chopped fresh parsley

In a large kettle, slowly sauté onions, garlic, and parsley in olive oil until onions are tender. Add water, and bring to a boil. Stir in rice, and boil, uncovered, for 15 minutes. Add cockles and boil 15 minutes more. Generously add salt and pepper to taste. Ladle into large soup bowls. Sprinkle with additional parsley. Makes 8 generous servings.

Art Treganza,
Airport Rescue Company No. 3

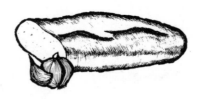

The predominant herb should be (and is) bay. Al Boccone's polenta technique is simpler and swifter than the traditional long-stirring method.

RABBIT WITH POLENTA PIEDMONTESE

1 dressed young rabbit (about 2½ pounds), cut into pieces
Flour seasoned well with salt and pepper
Olive oil
Bay-tomato sauce (recipe below)
Cheese polenta
Grated Parmesan cheese

Dust rabbit pieces with seasoned flour. Brown on all sides in olive oil in a Dutch oven or heavy kettle with cover; remove any excess oil. Pour bay-tomato sauce over rabbit. Cover and simmer for 45 minutes or until rabbit is tender. Serve rabbit with cheese polenta alongside. Spoon over polenta. Sprinkle with Parmesan. Makes 4 servings.

BAY-TOMATO SAUCE

Sauté 1 large onion, chopped, in 3 tablespoons olive oil until limp. Add 1 clove garlic, minced or mashed, and ¼ cup chopped fresh parsley, and sauté until coated with oil. Stir in 1 can (8 ounces) tomato sauce, 1 cup dry red wine, 1 bay leaf, ¼ teaspoon salt, ⅛ teaspoon coarsely ground black pepper, and ⅛ teaspoon mixed dry Italian herbs. Cover and simmer 20 minutes, stirring occasionally.

CHEESE POLENTA

Stirring constantly with a wire whisk, gradually add ¾ cup polenta (or cornmeal) to 3 cups boiling water with 1 teaspoon salt. Cook, stirring, for 5 minutes. Remove from heat and top with ½ pound Teleme or Monterey cream cheese, cut into small chunks. Bake in a moderate oven (350°) for 40 minutes or until set. Spoon out to serve.

Al Boccone, Engine Company No. 9

The firemen who know venison best say the best thing you can do to the tender steaks and chops is fry them fast to rare or medium-rare, and then salt and pepper them.

Dick Marracq discovered that the same treatment makes a glorious delicacy out of the fresh tenderloin muscle. To do it, you've got to get the tenderloin while it is fresh; if you wait until the meat hangs long enough for butchering, the tenderloin will have shrunk too much to be useful. Dick Marracq strips it out right at camp, and cooks it over the campfire for his fellow hunters.

VENISON TENDERLOIN MORSELS

2 whole fresh venison tenderloins
Shortening
Salt and pepper

Slice tenderloin crosswise into 2-inch pieces to resemble little cylinders. Stand on end and, with a cleaver, pound to flatten to a thin patty. Heat a generous amount of shortening in a heavy frying pan until very hot. Add tenderloin pieces and brown quickly on both sides. Season with salt and pepper. Makes about 3 servings.

Dick Marracq, Engine Company No. 34

OLIVE VENISON STEW

2 pounds venison stew meat, cut into
   1½-inch cubes
½ cup *each* vinegar and dry white wine
Flour seasoned well with salt and
   pepper
Bacon drippings
1 medium-sized onion, finely chopped
¼ cup chopped fresh parsley
⅛ teaspoon crumbled dried thyme
About 1 cup beef broth
1 cup dry white wine
½ pound medium-sized fresh mushrooms, halved
1 can (about 8 ounces) pitted black
   olives, drained

Marinate venison overnight in vinegar and ½ cup wine. Drain thoroughly and dry on paper towels. Coat with seasoned flour. Heat bacon drippings in a heavy pan with cover. Add meat, and brown quickly on all sides. When almost brown, add onion, and sauté until limp. Stir in parsley, thyme, and ½ cup *each* of the beef broth and wine. Cover and simmer for 1½ hours or until meat is almost tender. (Add beef broth as necessary to replace liquid lost by evaporation.) Add mushrooms, olives, and remaining wine. Cover and simmer 30 minutes more. (Thicken liquid, if you wish, with a *roux* made by blending equal parts butter and flour. Stir *roux* into stew liquid and cook, stirring, until juices thicken.) Taste and correct seasonings. Makes 6 servings.

Andy Dunn, Engine Company No. 20

Dick Marracq, his hunting dogs, and his huntsman friends head north—to Tule-lake or the Russian River country for duck, goose, pheasant, quail hunting. Years of hunting and cooking the quarry qualify him as an expert.

How to handle a tough goose.

WILD GOOSE SAUTÉ

Use just the breast and the little thighs. Separate breast, remove skin, and cut across the grain, into ½-inch-thick slices. Sprinkle breast pieces and thighs on both sides with garlic salt and pepper; let stand 1 hour. Dip breast pieces and thighs into beaten egg, coat with flour or cornmeal. Fry quickly in bacon fat, cooking thighs a little longer than breast meat. Sprinkle with fresh lemon juice.

Pheasant at the hunting camp.

PHEASANT BARBECUE

Cut pheasant in half. Salt and pepper. Place, bone side down, on grill over medium-hot coals, and cook about 20 minutes; turn and barbecue on flesh side about 10 minutes.

Pheasant at home.

WINE-STEAMED PHEASANT

Coat pheasant pieces in flour seasoned well with salt and pepper. Brown well in shortening. Place on rack in a large steaming kettle with 1 inch of dry white wine and a chopped onion in bottom. Cover tightly and steam pheasant for 1 hour or until tender. (Add more wine if necessary.)

"I like just the taste of duck. So I don't do too much to it. Just roast it — rare."

SIMPLY ROAST DUCK

Sprinkle duck cavity with salt and pepper; stuff with an apple quarter, an onion quarter, a parsley sprig, and a celery top. Rub outside with bacon fat, salt, and pepper. Place, breast side up, on rack in roasting pan. Roast in a very hot oven (450°) for 25 minutes (for a 1½-pound duck), 30 minutes (for a 2-pound duck), or 40 minutes (for a 3-pound duck).

Dick Marracq, Engine Company No. 34

John Bogue also spit-roasts quail (for about 35 minutes), using the same baste he recommends for oven roasting.

HERB-ROASTED QUAIL

Wash and dry quail and rub with olive oil. Sprinkle inside and out with salt and pepper. Place on rack in a shallow open roasting pan and bake in a very hot oven (450°) for 5 minutes. Meantime, make an herb basting paste in these proportions: ¼ cup olive oil; 1 small clove garlic, minced or mashed; ¼ teaspoon *each* crumbled dried oregano and rosemary. Reduce oven heat to slow (300°) and bake quail 25 minutes more, basting frequently with herb baste.

John Bogue, Sr., Engine Company No. 17

CHAPTER 10

vegetables

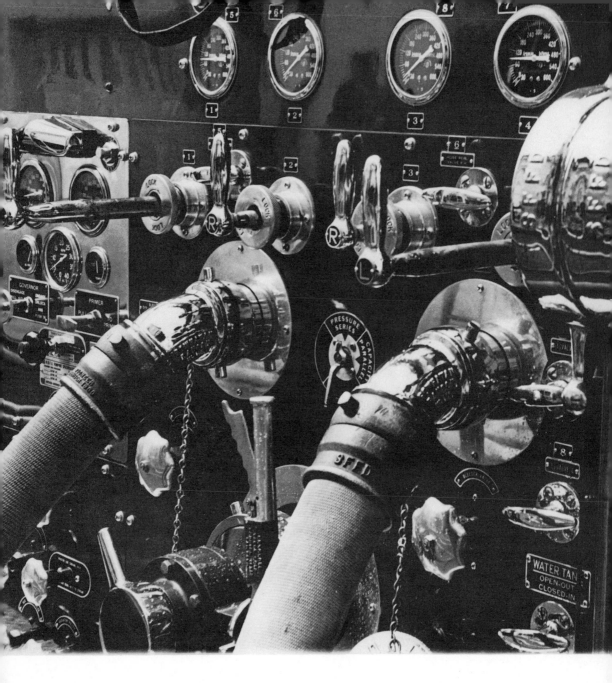

VEGETABLES

At some firehouses, they're so fond of vegetables, they grow their own in a plot in back of the firehouse. They do at Engine No. 19 and No. 15. And they used to at the airport.

Three kinds of crispness: fragile green pea pods, icy water chestnuts, toasted pumpkin seeds.

SUGAR PEAS CHINESE

4 tablespoons salad oil
1 pound Chinese snow peas (edible-pod or sugar peas), tips and strings removed, or 2 packages (7 ounces *each*) frozen pea pods
1 cup sliced water chestnuts
¾ teaspoon ground ginger
½ teaspoon salt
¼ teaspoon *each* sugar and monosodium glutamate
1/16 teaspoon pepper
About 4 tablespoons salted pumpkin or sunflower seed kernels

Heat salad oil over high heat in heavy frying pan. Add snow peas and water chestnuts; toss and cook over high heat for 1 minute. Add ginger, salt, sugar, monosodium glutamate, and pepper. Cover vegetables and cook over high heat for 2 minutes more, stirring once, or until just tender. Sprinkle with pumpkin seeds. Serve immediately. Makes 6 servings.

Russ McKlem, Engine Company No. 39

For a variation, add ¼ cup finely chopped walnuts to the butter sauce.

HERBED FIDDLE SQUASH

2 pounds crookneck yellow (summer) squash, cut in half lengthwise
Boiling salted water
4 tablespoons butter
2 teaspoons lemon juice
About ¼ teaspoon *each* salt and crumbled dried sweet basil
Dash of pepper

Cook squash, covered, in a small amount of boiling salted water until just tender, about 10 minutes. Meantime, melt butter, and stir in lemon juice, salt, basil, and pepper. Drain squash, turn into warm serving dish, and pour butter sauce over top. Makes 4 servings.

Larry Middendorf, Engine Company No. 5

Carrots are trumps for a firehouse cook; they're always inexpensive, always in season. Parsley mayonnaise makes a quick, sure dressing.

CARROTS MAYONNAISE

6 carrots, peeled, and sliced crosswise
Boiling salted water
Salt and pepper
¼ cup mayonnaise
1 tablespoon chopped fresh parsley
1 teaspoon lemon juice

Cook carrots, covered, in boiling salted water just until tender. Drain; season with salt and pepper. Combine mayonnaise, parsley, and lemon juice and toss lightly with hot carrots. Serve immediately. Makes 4 servings.

Ed Begley, Engine Company No. 2

When the summer's zucchini is fresh and abundant, Joe Everson makes this green-vegetable frittata for the vegetable side dish to meats.

HERBED ZUCCHINI FRITTATA

1 medium-sized onion, finely chopped
¼ teaspoon *each* crumbled dried rosemary and sweet basil
2 tablespoons butter
2½ pounds fresh zucchini, cooked and well drained
1 package (10 ounces) frozen chopped spinach, cooked and well drained
5 eggs
4 tablespoons grated Parmesan cheese
2 tablespoons fine dry bread crumbs
1¼ teaspoons salt
¼ teaspoon pepper

Add onion, rosemary, and sweet basil to melted butter in a frying pan, and sauté until onion is golden and tender. Combine zucchini and spinach in a mixing bowl, and beat with electric mixer to blend. Beat in eggs, one at a time. Add Parmesan, bread crumbs, salt, and pepper. Fold in sautéed onion. Turn into a buttered baking dish (about 1½ quarts) and bake in a moderate oven (350°) for 45 minutes or until set. Makes 8 servings.

Joe Everson, Engine Company No. 9

Ashley Hobson does these Sherried Limas for a luncheon main dish. He makes them hot with chili powder, so cut back on it if you prefer less heat.

SHERRIED LIMAS

1 large onion, chopped
¾ cup chopped green pepper
¼ cup olive oil
1 clove garlic, minced or mashed
1 can (about 1 pound) green lima
    beans, drained
1 can (about 4 ounces) chopped ripe
    olives, drained
1 can (8 ounces) tomato sauce
½ cup *each* grated Parmesan cheese
    and dry Sherry
1 tablespoon chili powder
¾ teaspoon salt
6 thin slices bacon

In a medium-large frying pan, sauté onions and green peppers in olive oil until limp. Add remaining ingredients except bacon; mix thoroughly. Arrange bacon slices over top. Bake, uncovered, in a moderate oven (350°) for 20 minutes. Makes 6 servings.

Ashley Hobson, Engine Company No. 40

Something John Bogue made up: "The fellows really like 'em; they say they taste like oysters."

CHARD STEM FRITTERS

White stems trimmed from 2 bunches
    Swiss chard
Boiling salted water
2 eggs
1½ teaspoons salt
¾ teaspoon crumbled dried marjoram
¼ teaspoon pepper
1 clove garlic
Fine dry bread crumbs
Oil for deep frying

Cut stems into about 3-inch pieces. Cook in boiling salted water until just tender; drain thoroughly and dry on paper towels. Beat eggs with salt, marjoram, pepper, and juice scraped from split clove of garlic. Dip stems into egg, then into bread crumbs. Let stand about 10 minutes. Drop stems into heated oil (380°) for deep frying. Fry until golden. Makes 6 servings.

John Bogue, Engine Company No. 17

LETTUCE BUTTERED
NEW POTATOES AND PEAS

1 pound very small unpeeled new potatoes, well scrubbed (or larger potatoes, peeled and cut into about
1½-inch pieces)
Boiling salted water
3 tablespoons butter
1 pound fresh peas, shelled (about 1
cup peas)
6 leaves butter or Boston lettuce,
broken into 1-inch squares
¾ teaspoon salt
¼ teaspoon pepper
2 tablespoons water
Fresh lemon juice

Cook potatoes in boiling salted water
until almost tender, about 10 minutes.
Drain. Melt butter in a pan with cover.
Add potatoes, and stir gently to coat
with butter. Add peas, lettuce, salt,
pepper, and water. Cover and cook
over medium heat for about 15 minutes or until vegetables are tender;
gently stir occasionally. Just before
serving, sprinkle lightly with lemon
juice. Makes 4 servings.

Herb Muzio, Engine Company No. 44

MUSTARD BEANS AMANDINE

1¼ pounds fresh green beans
Boiling salted water
¼ pound fresh mushrooms, very thinly
sliced
6 tablespoons butter
½ cup slivered almonds
1 tablespoon lemon juice
½ teaspoon *each* dry mustard and
onion salt
Dash of pepper

Sliver beans lengthwise. Cook, covered, in boiling salted water until barely
tender, about 10 minutes. Drain and
add mushrooms. Meantime, in a small
pan, lightly brown butter and almonds
over low heat, stirring occasionally. Stir
in lemon juice, mustard, onion salt, and
pepper. Pour over beans and mushrooms, and heat through. Makes 6
servings.

Herb Muzio, Engine Company No. 44

Use any large winter baking squash, but John Hearne designed the recipe for banana squash. For spice amounts, he says, "Sprinkle with a good layer of cinnamon; don't be bashful with it. Less nutmeg."

SUGAR-SCORED BAKED SQUASH

Banana squash, cut into serving-size
  pieces
Soft butter
Ground cinnamon
Ground nutmeg
Brown sugar

With a sharp knife, score squash flesh about every ½ inch, cutting both crosswise and lengthwise of the flesh and almost to but not through rind. Spread butter thickly over top and sides of each piece. Sprinkle very generously with cinnamon; sprinkle with nutmeg. Sprinkle lightly with brown sugar. Place in a shallow baking pan and bake in a moderate oven (375°) for 1 hour.

John Hearne, Engine Company No. 9

For perfect Deviled Sprouts à la John Hearne: Cook sprouts until they're "still a little on the crisp side." Drain them well ("shake the daylights out of 'em").

DEVILED SPROUTS

½ cup butter
4 tablespoons snipped fresh chives
1 tablespoon prepared mustard
1 teaspoon Worcestershire sauce
⅛ teaspoon *each* garlic powder and
  pepper
Dash of celery salt
2 pounds Brussels sprouts
Boiling salted water

Make devil sauce: Melt butter in a small saucepan, and stir in chives, mustard, Worcestershire, garlic powder, pepper, and celery salt. Simmer, uncovered, for 30 minutes, stirring occasionally. Clean and trim sprouts and cook, covered, in a small amount of boiling salted water until barely tender, about 8 minutes. Drain sprouts well, return to warm pan, pour devil sauce over them, and place over low heat. Turn sprouts in sauce (handling them gently with 2 spoons) until well coated and heated through. Makes 6 servings.

John Hearne, Engine Company No. 9

Lloyd Chambers is an experimental cook. He'll try anything once—at the firehouse, where he's got a captive audience.

Try this with spareribs or frankfurters.

SAUTERNE SAUERKRAUT

1 large can (1 pound, 12 ounces) sauerkraut, well drained
1 medium-sized onion, very finely chopped
2 apples, peeled, cored, and coarsely grated
1 cup dry Sauterne
½ teaspoon caraway seeds (optional)

Combine all ingredients in a saucepan and heat slowly, stirring occasionally, for about 20 minutes or until onions are tender. Makes 6 servings.

Lloyd Chambers, Truck Company No. 14

SOUR CREAMED BRUSSELS SPROUTS

2 medium-sized onions, finely chopped
½ cup butter
1 cup sour cream
¼ teaspoon salt
Dash of pepper
2 pounds fresh Brussels sprouts (or 2 packages, 10 ounces *each,* frozen sprouts)
Boiling salted water
Ground nutmeg

Sauté onions in butter over low heat, stirring, until deep golden, about 30 minutes. Keeping heat very low, stir in sour cream, salt, and pepper. Meantime, cook sprouts, covered, in boiling salted water until tender; drain well. Add to onion sauce and turn gently to mix. Sprinkle very lightly with nutmeg. Serve immediately. Makes 6 servings.

Lloyd Chambers, Truck Company No. 14

Possibly it's his French heritage that accounts for Mel Lavoie's finesse with foods. Possibly, partly, his appreciative firehouse audience. Praise for his cooking runs along these lines:

"He's as good a cook as you'll ever find."

"He's got more recipes than anyone in the world."

"It's not just the cooking with Mel; it's the layout, the atmosphere he provides. Why, he'll even make individual salads for twelve men!"

POTATOES LAVOIE

4 medium-sized baking potatoes
¼ pound bacon, finely diced
1 medium-sized onion, finely chopped
Milk
Salt and pepper
3 tablespoons butter

Scrub potatoes, rub skins with oil, and bake in a hot oven (400°) for 1 hour or until tender. Meantime, sauté bacon in frying pan until crisp; remove bacon. Add onions to frying pan, and sauté until golden. Pour off excess drippings. Cut baked potatoes in half, lengthwise; scoop out centers and whip with enough milk to make them fluffy. Add bacon, onion, and salt and pepper to taste; and whip again. Refill shells with potato mixture. Place on baking sheet. Dot tops with butter. Bake in a very hot oven (500°) for 10 minutes or until brown. Makes 4 to 8 servings.

Mel Lavoie, Engine Company No. 8

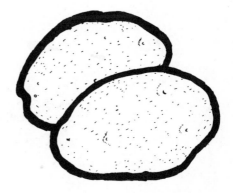

For an oven dinner.

CARROT STRIP CASSEROLE

6 medium-sized carrots
¾ cup water
Scant ¾ teaspoon salt
3 tablespoons butter
Finely chopped fresh parsley

Peel carrots and cut in half crosswise; slice lengthwise into strips about ³⁄₁₆ inch thick; place in casserole (1 quart) with cover. Add water, sprinkle carrots with salt, dot with butter. Cover. Bake in a moderate oven (350°) for 35 minutes or until tender. Sprinkle with parsley. Makes 6 servings.

Bob Hinman, Engine Company No. 26

FRENCH LETTUCE PEAS

1 package (10 ounces) frozen peas
Boiling salted water
⅓ cup finely chopped head lettuce
2 green onions, white part only, finely minced
2 tablespoons butter
½ teaspoon sugar
Salt

Cook peas in boiling salted water until almost tender. Drain off water. Stir in lettuce, onions, butter, and sugar; cover, and cook over high heat for just a few minutes, until lettuce and onions are limp. Salt to taste. Makes 4 servings.

Mel Lavoie, Engine Company No. 8

Eggplant out of the garden becomes Gazonk Eggplant at Engine No. 39—in the hands of Russ McKlem. It's a fresh-tasting dish for all its rich-sounding ingredients; the thin onion rings stay sweetly crisp.

(Gazonk seems to be anything that is undefined.)

GAZONK EGGPLANT

1 large eggplant, unpeeled
Flour
Salad oil
Bacon-tomato sauce
1 large onion, very thinly sliced and separated into rings
½ pound sharp Cheddar cheese, sliced
¼ cup dry white wine
About ¼ teaspoon *each* salt, pepper, and monosodium glutamate
3 to 4 tablespoons wheat germ

Cut eggplant into crosswise slices ⅛ -to- ¼ -inch thick. Coat slices with flour, and brown quickly on both sides in heated oil in frying pan. Arrange one layer of eggplant over bottom of baking dish (about 2 quarts). Spoon over enough bacon-tomato sauce to cover, sprinkle with onion rings, top with cheese. Repeat layering of eggplant, tomato sauce, onion, and cheese to use all ingredients. Sprinkle with wine, salt, pepper, and monosodium glutamate. Top with wheat germ. Bake, uncovered, in a moderate oven (350°) for 20 to 25 minutes.

BACON-TOMATO SAUCE

Combine in a saucepan 1 large can (1 pound, 12 ounces) solid-pack tomatoes; 6 slices bacon, cooked until crisp and crumbled; ¼ teaspoon salt; ⅛ teaspoon *each* pepper and crumbled dried rosemary, thyme, and oregano. Cook, uncovered, stirring occasionally until well blended and reduced slightly, about 45 minutes. (Break large tomato pieces into small ones.)

Russ McKlem, Engine Company No. 39

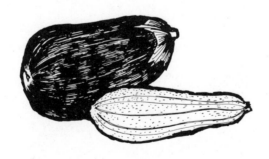

Sometimes, Frank Rey treats the men to a luxurious vegetable side dish—sautéed mushrooms. The first step of preparation: "Get the mushrooms when they're cheap."

MUSHROOM-WINE SAUTÉ

1 pound medium-sized mushrooms
About 6 tablespoons olive oil
Salt and freshly ground black pepper
2 tablespoons dry red wine
3 tablespoons chopped fresh parsley
1 small clove garlic, minced or mashed

Wash mushrooms quickly in cold water (don't soak); drain, dry, trim off end of stems, slice in half. (If mushrooms are not uniform in size, slice large ones into three pieces, leave button mushrooms whole.) Heat olive oil in a medium-sized frying pan. Add mushrooms, cover, and cook over medium-high heat for about 10 minutes or until well browned. (Stir frequently; pour off excess liquid as it accumulates.) Season mushrooms with salt and pepper. Reduce heat; add wine, parsley, and garlic; cook and stir about 3 minutes more. Makes 4 servings.

Frank Rey, Engine Company No. 27

CHAPTER 11

pastas and sauces, rice, gnocchi, baked beans

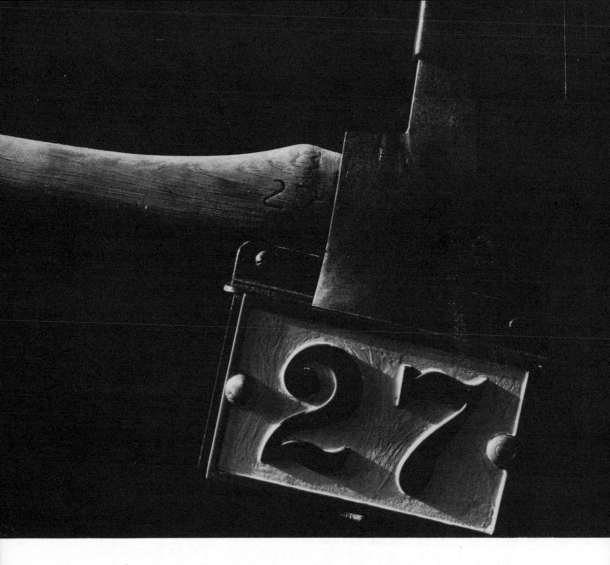

PASTAS AND SAUCES, RICE, GNOCCHI, BAKED BEANS

The purpose of a pasta meal is more often magnificent eating than firehouse budget control, though sometimes the latter is a side benefit—if the chef's pasta sauce isn't too extravagant with costly cheeses and sausages, rare spices, imported mushrooms . . . (an unlikelihood). And sometimes a fine pasta saves Friday from fish.

A firehouse side dish rates as much regard as the main dish: an Armenian pours his energies into priming his perfect pilaff, an Italian his risotto, a Spaniard his rice. . . . Some say the fireman-and-family summer steak barbecues are less for the sake of the steak than for the traditional grand kettle of savory beans.

Before William F. Murray was appointed Chief of the Department, he was sometimes the cook at Truck No. 13. His specialty: a terrific Italian gravy for pasta. He used it on spaghetti and passed freshly grated Parmesan cheese to be sprinkled on. Use it on your favorite pasta.

(Tradition carried on, and now Jack Sherry uses that same lovely sauce as the sauce and baste for the rare roast beef on page 47.)

CHIEF MURRAY'S ITALIAN GRAVY

3 large onions, chopped
¼ cup salad oil
½ cup finely chopped fresh parsley
4 cloves garlic, minced or mashed
2 hot, spicy Italian link sausages (about ⅓ pound), cut from casings and crumbled
1 pound ground chuck
4 cans (8 ounces *each*) tomato sauce
2 cups water
½ cup dry red wine
1 to 2 ounces dried mushrooms, soaked, squeezed dry, and finely chopped
1 teaspoon salt
¼ teaspoon coarsely ground black pepper
⅛ teaspoon crumbled dried rosemary
1/16 teaspoon poultry seasoning

In a frying pan, sauté onions in salad oil just until limp. Add parsley and garlic, and sauté just until coated with oil. In a large pan, slowly brown sausages; add chuck and brown. Add to meat the onion mixture and remaining ingredients. Cover loosely and simmer, stirring occasionally, for 3 hours. Skim off any excess oil. Makes about 2 quarts sauce.

William F. Murray,
Chief of the San Francisco Fire Department

For Friday nights.

GREEN-PEPPERED CLAM SPAGHETTI

2 medium-sized onions, finely chopped
2 medium-sized green bell peppers, chopped
½ teaspoon mixed Italian dry herbs
6 tablespoons butter
2 cans (7½ ounces *each*) minced clams
12 ounces vermicelli or spaghetti, cooked and drained
Grated Parmesan cheese

Slowly sauté onions, peppers, and mixed Italian herbs in butter, stirring occasionally, until onions are golden and peppers tender. Add clams with clam liquor and cook slowly, uncovered, for 15 minutes more; stir occasionally. Pour over hot pasta on a heated serving platter. Sprinkle very generously with Parmesan. Makes 4 servings.

Charlie Radford, Engine Company No. 32

Three cheeses combine to make an elegant macaroni and cheese.

MACARONI MORNAY

1 large onion, finely chopped
½ cup *each* chopped green bell pepper and finely chopped fresh parsley
3 eggs, beaten
2 teaspoons prepared mustard
Mornay sauce
12 ounces elbow macaroni, cooked, rinsed, and drained
About 2 cups shredded sharp Cheddar cheese

Stir onion, green pepper, parsley, eggs, and mustard into Mornay sauce. Fold in macaroni. Turn into a buttered casserole (about 2 quarts). Sprinkle with Cheddar cheese. Bake in a moderate oven (350°) for 30 minutes. Makes 10 servings.

MORNAY SAUCE

Melt 3 tablespoons butter in a saucepan. Stir in 3 tablespoons flour to make a smooth paste. Gradually add 3 cups milk, cooking and stirring until sauce is slightly thickened and smooth. Stir in ½ cup *each* shredded Swiss and shredded or grated Parmesan cheese, 3 teaspoons salt, 1 teaspoon Worcestershire sauce, ½ teaspoon ground nutmeg, and about ½ teaspoon ground black pepper.

Ashley Hobson, Engine Company No. 40

An Italian grandmother from the region of Abruzzi taught Richard Paganelli how to make this spectacular sauce of meat balls and sausages.

Get the sausages from an Italian sausagemaker; it's best to get half of the sweet spicy sausages, half of the hot spicy ones. (If you can't get authentic fresh Italian sausages, you can substitute spicy link pork sausages; you'll have a fine spaghetti sauce, but not Abruzzi.)

SPAGHETTI SAUCE ABRUZZI

1 medium-sized onion, chopped
1 tablespoon salad oil
2 cloves garlic, minced or mashed
1 large can (1 pound, 12 ounces) Italian-style peeled whole tomatoes
1 can (6 ounces) tomato paste
⅓ cup water and ⅓ cup water from soaking mushrooms
½ to 1 ounce Italian dry mushrooms, soaked in water until tender, squeezed dry, and thinly sliced
1 teaspoon sugar
1 ounce salt pork, cut into very small pieces
2 pounds spicy fresh Italian link sausages
1½ pounds ground chuck
¼ pound imported Romano cheese, grated
1 egg
⅔ cup chopped fresh parsley
¾ teaspoon *each* salt and freshly ground black pepper

In a large kettle, sauté onions in salad oil until limp. Stir in garlic, tomatoes, tomato paste, water, water from soaking mushrooms, mushrooms, and sugar. Cover loosely and place over low heat. Meantime, in a frying pan, brown salt pork and add, with drippings, to tomato sauce. Brown sausages in their own fat, pouring off excess fat as it accumulates; add sausages to tomato sauce. Mix together ground chuck, cheese, egg, parsley, salt, and black pepper. Form into meat balls the size of a walnut. Brown on all sides, and add to tomato sauce. Cover sauce loosely and simmer, stirring frequently, for 2 to 3 hours, until cooked down to a rich sauce. Skim off excess fat. Serve over hot cooked spaghetti. Makes sauce for about 8 servings.

Richard Paganelli, Engine Company No. 17

Al Boccone knows pastas intimately—how to cook them, how to sauce them, where to buy them, fresh and dry, with egg and without, tagliarini, mostaccioli, linguini, farfallette. . . . His cardinal rule: cook pastas *al dente*. "You offend pasta when you overcook it."

On some Friday nights, he does this take-off on Fettuccine—sour cream and salted butter instead of sweet. The mushrooms are optional.

SOUR CREAM FETTUCCINE

½ pound mushrooms, sliced
3 tablespoons olive oil
Salt and freshly ground black pepper
2 large cloves garlic, crushed
1 cup butter
1 cup *each* finely chopped fresh parsley, sour cream, and grated Parmesan cheese
1 pound fresh (or ¾ pound dried) tagliarini (or other pasta)
Additional freshly ground black pepper and Parmesan

Sauté mushrooms in olive oil until tender; season with salt and pepper. Heat garlic in melted butter until it turns golden; remove garlic; stir in parsley. Pour hot parsley butter, sautéed mushrooms, sour cream, and Parmesan over hot tagliarini, stirring as you add. Mix thoroughly. Serve immediately. Offer black pepper and additional Parmesan. Makes 4 to 6 servings.

Al Boccone, Engine Company No. 9

When it's spring, and the first fresh *basilico* comes into the North Beach markets, it's time for the Genoese Italians to make pesto—and a feast of fresh Tagliarini con Pesto. (They say, when it comes to pesto, "There's no such thing as a little bit of garlic.")

Lest anyone think that the cream cheese ingredient is an American addition to pesto, Al Boccone reassures that the recipe came from a good cook right from Genoa (the home of pesto) and the American cream cheese corresponds to an Italian cheese.

TAGLIARINI CON PESTO

1 bunch fresh basil (leaves only)
About 2 tablespoons olive oil
1 large clove garlic
About ⅛ teaspoon salt
About ¹⁄₁₆ teaspoon coarsely ground
   black pepper
About 1 ounce cream cheese, softened
½ cup butter
1 large clove garlic, crushed
About 2 green onions with part of the
   green tops, finely chopped (optional)
About 1 cup chopped fresh parsley
1 pound fresh tagliarini, cooked
   al dente and drained
About ¾ cup grated Parmesan cheese
Additional Parmesan

Put basil, oil, one clove of garlic, salt, and pepper in blender container, and whirl until smooth. (You should have a fairly thick paste, loose enough to pour.) Add cream cheese and whirl again. Meantime, heat butter with crushed garlic until garlic is golden; discard garlic. Add onions and parsley to butter and just heat through. Pour hot butter mixture over tagliarini, then basil mixture, then Parmesan, mixing as you add. Serve immediately. Pass additional Parmesan. Makes about 4 servings.

Al Boccone, Engine Company No. 9

Frank Rey's version is simpler:

PESTO

Whirl together in a blender 4 parts fresh *basilico* leaves to 1 part fresh parsley (measure basil leaves and parsley sprigs), some olive oil, and salt, pepper, and fresh garlic to taste. Just before serving (and here's the trick that brings out a wonderful flavor), beat in a raw egg (use one egg for a large batch). Pour over hot, drained pasta, and sprinkle with grated Parmesan cheese.

Frank Rey, Engine Company No. 27

Lieutenant MacCarthy says the success of this dish is in the sauce.

The recipe is given in party proportions.

MEAT BALL SAUCE LASAGNE

Meat ball sauce
1 pound wide lasagne noodles, cooked, rinsed, and drained
1 pound Mozzarella cheese, cut into small cubes
½ pound Ricotta cheese
¼ cup grated Parmesan cheese

Remove meat balls from sauce. Plan for four layers of lasagne, three layers *each* of meat balls, Mozzarella, and Ricotta cheese. Spoon a little of the sauce over bottom of a baking pan (about 12 by 15 inches). Arrange one layer of lasagne over bottom of pan. Top with a layer of meat balls, then sauce, Mozzarella cheese, and Ricotta cheese. Repeat layering twice more. Top with a layer of lasagne and pour over remaining sauce. Sprinkle with Parmesan. Bake in a moderate oven (375°) for 1 hour. Cut into large squares. Makes 12 servings.

MEAT BALL SAUCE

Mix together thoroughly 3 pounds ground chuck; 1 medium-sized onion, minced; 1 large potato, finely grated; ½ green bell pepper, finely chopped; 2 teaspoons salt, and ¼ teaspoon pepper. Form into 1-inch balls; slowly brown on all sides in their own fat. Drain on paper towels. Meantime, combine in a Dutch oven or large kettle with cover 6 cans (8 ounces *each*) tomato sauce; 5 cups water; ¼ cup grated Parmesan cheese; 6 large pieces dried mushrooms, broken into small pieces; and ⅛ teaspoon crumbled dried oregano. Sauté ½ a green pepper, finely chopped, and 1 large onion, finely chopped, in 2 tablespoons salad oil until limp; drain on paper towels and add to tomato sauce. Add browned meat balls to tomato sauce. Cover loosely, and simmer for 3 to 4 hours; stir occasionally. Add salt and pepper to taste.

Lieutenant E. L. MacCarthy,
Airport Company No. 1

Make this to go with Scaloppine Lamb Shanks (page 56) or a roast chicken.

SAFFRON RISOTTO

4 tablespoons butter
1 cup long grain white rice
½ cup finely sliced green onions with part of green tops
Pinch of saffron
2 cups boiling chicken broth
½ cup grated Parmesan cheese
Salt and pepper to taste

Melt 3 tablespoons of the butter in a heavy pan with cover. Add rice, onions, and saffron, and cook, stirring, until rice is golden and onions tender. Stir in chicken broth; cover and cook over very low heat for 18 minutes or until rice is barely tender. Dot with remaining butter, sprinkle with cheese, toss to mix thoroughly, correct seasoning, and serve immediately. Makes 4 servings.

Al Boccone, Engine Company No. 9

Armenian Jack Kermoian not only gets superlative results when he cooks; he knows the reason why: in this pilaff, the vermicelli holds the butter, then releases it to mingle with rice during steaming. This buttery pilaff is good with almost all meats, exceptional with Sherry Shish Kebab (see page 103).

KERMOIAN'S ARMENIAN PILAFF

¼ cup butter
½ cup finely broken vermicelli (pasta)
1 cup long grain white rice
2 cups boiling beef broth
Salt and pepper to taste

Melt butter in a heavy saucepan with cover. Add broken vermicelli, and cook, stirring, until it browns slightly. Add rice, and cook 2 or 3 minutes, stirring, until coated with butter. Stir in boiling beef stock, salt, and pepper. Cover and simmer for 20 minutes. Makes 4 generous servings.

Jack Kermoian, Engine Company No. 15

At the firehouse, squares of this rice torta, served hot with a pat of butter melting on top, go with roast meats. In private life, Frank Rey makes torta in quantity for a big Italian family picnic feast; then it's served cold.

GREEN RICE TORTA

1 cup long grain white rice, cooked just until tender and cooled
1 bunch (1 pound) Swiss chard, cooked until tender, drained with all moisture squeezed out, and finely chopped
⅓ cup *each* grated Parmesan cheese and finely chopped fresh parsley
1 clove garlic, minced or mashed
½ teaspoon *each* salt and coarsely ground black pepper
2 eggs, beaten
Olive oil
About 2 tablespoons fine dry bread crumbs

Mix together the rice, Swiss chard, Parmesan, parsley, garlic, salt, pepper, and eggs. Grease an 8-inch-square baking pan with olive oil. Add bread crumbs, and shake to coat bottom and sides of pan. Turn in rice mixture. Bake in a slow oven (325°) for 30 minutes. Cut into squares or rectangles. Serve hot or cold. Makes 8 servings.

Frank Rey, Engine Company No. 27

The Spanish Rice that accompanies enchiladas is just as important as they are themselves. Jack Sherry is certain that no other fireman can make this simple and perfect Spanish Rice. Because, up to now, he's guarded the recipe jealously—even from his cooking associates.

He got the recipe from Spain, by way of Texas, so it's supposed to be authentic. The important technique: brown the rice thoroughly.

SHERRY'S SPANISH RICE

¼ pound bacon, diced
2 medium-sized onions, finely chopped
1 green bell pepper, chopped
2 cups long grain white rice
1¼ teaspoons salt
¼ teaspoon pepper
1 large can (1 pound, 12 ounces) solid-
   pack tomatoes, broken up

In a large frying pan, cook bacon slowly; when partially cooked, pour off ¼ cup of the accumulated drippings into another pan. Add onions and peppers to bacon, and sauté until limp. Add rice to bacon drippings and heat, stirring, until rice is toasted golden and thoroughly coated with oil. Stir in salt and pepper, sautéed vegetables, and tomatoes. Turn into casserole (about 2½ quarts), cover tightly, and bake in a slow oven (325°) for 40 minutes. Makes 12 servings.

Jack Sherry, Truck Company No. 3

Anyone who doubts the finesse of firehouse cooking should taste these airy drifts of potato. It's nearly an all-day's project to make them for one of the biggest companies of the city—Engine No. 1. Art Mazzuchi learned how to make them by watching his mother.

Serve gnocchi with roast beef or pot roast and top both with a good beef gravy.

POTATO GNOCCHI

3 medium-sized potatoes (dry, mealy type)
About 1 cup flour
1 egg
1½ teaspoons salt
Additional flour
Boiling salted water with oil

Boil unpeeled potatoes until tender. Peel while hot. Put into a mixing bowl, and begin mashing immediately, adding flour a little at a time while potatoes are hot. Mash or beat until almost smooth. When mixture has cooled partially, add egg and salt, and mix until smooth. Turn mixture out onto a well-floured board. Knead, working in more flour as necessary, to form a smooth, fairly soft, nonsticky dough. Divide dough into several parts, and shape each into a log about ⅝ inch in diameter. Cut into 1½-inch pieces. With tines of a floured fork, scribe each piece of dough so it curls. Place in a single layer on waxed paper. Sprinkle lightly with flour. Cook immediately or allow to stand for as long as 2 hours. Add about one-third of the gnocchi at a time to a large kettle of boiling salted water with a little oil added (water should not stop boiling). Cook about 5 minutes. Drain, and keep warm in a heated bowl until all have been cooked. Makes 6 servings.

Art Mazzuchi, Engine Company No. 1

Andy Dunn baked a great pot of beans when he was at old Engine Company No. 31 at the corner of Green and Leavenworth. Part of his talent was procuring the lean, well-smoked bacon from a fine old sausage house just down the street. (He knew the owner.)

ANDY DUNN'S BEANS

2 cups small white dry beans
Water
2 large onions, sliced
½ pound very lean bacon slices
⅔ cup dark corn syrup
4 teaspoons dry mustard
About 1½ teaspoons salt
About ½ teaspoon pepper

Wash beans, cover with cold water, and soak overnight. Drain. Put beans and onions into a large kettle with fresh water to cover. Bring to a boil, then simmer, covered, for 1 hour or just until tender. Drain, reserving liquid. Cut half the bacon into small pieces and add to beans along with syrup, mustard, salt, pepper, and 1 cup of the reserved liquid. Turn into a pot or casserole (about 2½ quarts); top with remaining bacon strips; cover and bake in a slow oven (300°) for 1½ hours. Remove cover and bake 30 minutes more. (If necessary, add more liquid.) Makes 6 to 8 servings.

Andy Dunn, Engine Company No. 20

These are rather refined Chili Beans—with only a latent snap of hotness. The seasonings blend to mellowness.

CHILI BEANS

1 pound (about 2 cups) dry pinto beans
Water
1 pound ground chuck
1 large onion, chopped
1 small can (1 pound) stewed tomatoes
1 small can (10 ounces) red chili sauce
¼ cup vinegar
1 tablespoon chili powder
Dash of liquid hot pepper seasoning
Salt and pepper

Cover beans with cold water, cover, bring to a boil, then simmer for 3 hours. (Add water if necessary.) In a frying pan, slowly brown ground beef; when crumbly, add onion, and sauté until limp; add to beans along with remaining ingredients except salt and pepper. Cover and simmer for three hours or until beans are tender and liquid cooked down to consistency desired. (Cook uncovered if necessary to reduce liquid.) Add salt and pepper to taste. Makes 8 servings.

Charlie Radford, Engine Company No. 32

CHAPTER 12

sunday brunch and breakfast

SUNDAY BRUNCH AND BREAKFAST

Usually firemen eat breakfast at home before they start their 24-hour watch. But on Sundays it's different. Then, in most firehouses, it's the policy to have a big Sunday brunch—about eleven—instead of lunch.

Sometimes a fireman cooks breakfast—when he "works over a watch" (trades with someone and works two days in a row).

Larry Middendorf is a Sunday brunch specialist—as testify his Brunch Beer Buttermilk Pancakes, Brunch Frittata, and French Toast Eggplant.

He bakes Sunday morning Beer Buttermilk Pancakes by his father's recipe, but without the bacon fat his father added (Larry uses melted butter instead). These are light and puffy and with a delectable combined tang of beer, buttermilk, and sour cream. Favorite toppings: fresh strawberry (or other berry) preserves or a fresh batch of applesauce, still a little chunky, thickened with cornstarch and topped with sour cream.

These are obviously men's pancakes: they're supposed to be baked saucer size.

For a Sunday morning breakfast, Larry starts with a whole 2-pound box of buttermilk pancake mix, and calls on other ingredients in equally large proportions: a dozen eggs, a pint of sour cream, a quart of buttermilk, a can of beer. For family proportions, start more sparingly:

BEER BUTTERMILK PANCAKES

3 eggs
1 cup buttermilk
⅓ cup beer
½ cup sour cream
2 tablespoons melted butter
1½ cups buttermilk pancake mix

In a mixing bowl, beat eggs slightly, and beat in buttermilk, beer, sour cream, and melted butter. Add pancake mix, and beat until almost smooth. Spoon out into saucer-size circles on medium-hot ungreased griddle or heavy frying pan. Bake until golden brown on both sides (turn when bubbles appear all over on moist surface). Serve hot with topping of your choice. Makes about 18 pancakes.

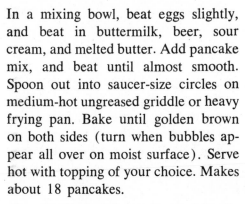

Larry Middendorf, Engine Company No. 5

The onions and green peppers taste sweet and fresh; the eggs bake golden over the top.

LARRY MIDDENDORF'S BRUNCH FRITTATA

1 medium-sized onion, chopped
½ large green bell pepper, chopped
2 tablespoons butter
1 dozen eggs
1 cup milk
⅜ teaspoon salt
⅛ teaspoon ground black pepper

Sauté onion and green pepper in butter just until limp. Beat eggs thoroughly with milk, salt, and pepper, and pour into a buttered baking pan (about 8 inches square). Spoon sautéed vegetables over top. Bake in a moderate oven (350°) for 45 minutes. Cut into squares or rectangles. Makes 6 servings.

Larry Middendorf, Engine Company No. 5

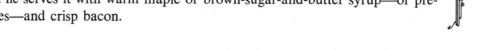

Larry Middendorf fries eggplant as his mother did, and that's like French toast. And he serves it with warm maple or brown-sugar-and-butter syrup—or preserves—and crisp bacon.

FRENCH TOAST EGGPLANT

1 large unpeeled eggplant, cut into ⅜-inch-thick crosswise slices
Salt
Flour
2 eggs, well beaten
Butter
Warm maple syrup (or preserves of your choice)

Sprinkle eggplant slices with salt. Dip in flour to coat, then into beaten egg. In a large frying pan, sauté slowly in melted butter until tender and crisp and golden brown on both sides. Pass maple syrup. Makes about 3 brunch servings.

Larry Middendorf, Engine Company No. 5

Ed McIntyre's mother brought the recipe for "Tattie Scones" from Scotland. Ed makes these crisp-crusted little potato scones for a firehouse Sunday morning—to go with ham and eggs, or bacon and eggs, and coffee. Serve scones hot, and melt in lots of butter and jelly.

SCOTTISH BREAKFAST POTATO SCONES

2 cups leftover mashed potatoes, well
   seasoned
Milk
About 1 cup flour
Shortening
Butter and jelly

Beat potatoes in a mixing bowl with enough milk to make them of a soft whipped consistency. Gradually add flour, mixing with a fork, to make a soft moist dough that pulls away from sides of bowl. Turn dough onto a well-floured sheet of waxed paper. Roll into a ball, coating surface with flour. With a floured rolling pin, roll dough out to a circle about ¼ inch thick. With a sharp knife, cut into quarter wedges. Heat enough shortening to generously cover bottom of a heavy frying pan. With a spatula, lift scones into frying pan; fry over medium-high heat until golden brown and crisp on both sides. Butter generously and serve while hot. Pass jelly. Makes 8 scones or 4 servings.

Ed McIntyre, Engine Company No. 3

At Engine No. 2, Jim King is the undisputed breakfast chef whenever anyone works over a watch.

One tradition is potato pancakes—with bacon and eggs. Another is Florentine Eggs—with ham slices juicy in crushed pineapple.

There's still a secret to this recipe that Jim King frankly refuses to disclose . . . something about the sauce. But even without that guarded secret cooked in, these Florentine Eggs are well worth trying. You "bake 'em easy" (in a 325° oven) and, in the same oven, heat thin ham slices in crushed pineapple.

SUNDAY EGGS FLORENTINE

3 packages (10 ounces *each*) frozen chopped spinach, cooked and drained
8 eggs
Salt and pepper
1 large can (14½ ounces) evaporated milk
2 cups (½ pound) shredded sharp Cheddar cheese
2 tablespoons grated onion
1½ cups sourdough French or other bread crumbs tossed with 4 table-spoons melted butter

Spread spinach in bottom of a shallow baking dish. With a fork, form 8 nests in spinach; drop an egg into each. Sprinkle spinach and eggs with salt and pepper to taste. Meantime, heat milk and cheese over hot water in top of a double boiler until cheese melts; stir in onions. Pour hot cheese sauce over eggs and spinach. Sprinkle with buttered crumbs. Bake in a moderate oven (350°) for 25 minutes. Makes 8 servings.

Jim King, Engine Company No. 2

Hopefully, there will be enough corned beef left from a dinner so Joe Everson will make his corned beef hash—for breakfast or supper.

COUNTRY CORNED BEEF AND EGGS

1 large onion, finely chopped
3 tablespoons butter
2 cups coarsely ground cooked
   corned beef
1½ cups coarsely chopped cooked
   potatoes
¼ cup finely chopped fresh parsley
Salt and coarsely ground black pepper
4 eggs

Sauté onion in butter until limp. Mix with corned beef, potatoes, parsley, and salt and a generous amount of pepper to taste. Spread in a buttered shallow baking pan (about 8 inches square). With back of a spoon, shape 4 nests for eggs. Bake in a slow oven (300°) for 20 minutes. Break an egg into each indentation; season lightly with salt and pepper. Return to oven and bake 20 minutes more or until eggs are set. Makes 4 servings.

Joe Everson, Engine Company No. 9

The size? "So they fit four in a pan."

CHIVED POTATO PANCAKES

3 eggs
1 tablespoon flour
1½ teaspoons salt
4 large new white potatoes, peeled and
   coarsely shredded
3 tablespoons snipped fresh chives
Salad oil

Beat eggs with a fork in a mixing bowl. Gradually add flour and salt, and beat until smooth. Add potatoes and chives, and mix thoroughly. Heat enough salad oil in a frying pan just to cover bottom of pan. Spoon potato mixture into hot frying pan; flatten slightly. Bake over medium-high heat until crisply brown on edges; turn and brown on second side. Makes 6 to 8 servings.

Jim King, Engine Company No. 2

Doug Robbins says this is good to whip up in the hungry hours of early morning when the fresh eggs are delivered to the firehouse.

SWISS AND NUTMEG OMELET

2 slices bacon
2 eggs
½ cup (about 2 ounces) shredded natural Swiss cheese
Nutmeg

In a small frying pan (about 7 inches), cook bacon until very crisp, drain, and crumble. Pour off all but about 1 tablespoon of the bacon grease remaining in frying pan. Beat eggs until light and fluffy, and pour into hot bacon grease in frying pan. Cook like a regular omelet, lifting cooked portions, and allowing uncooked portion to flow to bottom of pan. As omelet cooks, sprinkle bacon crumbles and Swiss cheese down center. Fold and turn onto warm plate, sprinkle lightly with nutmeg, and serve immediately. Makes 1 serving.

Doug Robbins, Engine Company No. 3

CHAPTER 13

miscellaneous, spontaneous

MISCELLANEOUS, SPONTANEOUS

The firehouse lunch, a 3 A.M. snack, a distinguished garlic bread, the enchilada enthusiasm, a stupendous pie, the Irish breads.

Lunch can be many things—or anything. Some houses have order and discipline and expectation about lunch; others are utterly haphazard. Whatever the lunch, it's simple, not time consuming—perhaps fresh ravioli from North Beach, hamburgers quickly fried, sandwiches from a corner delicatessen, a sturdy soup—or maybe a big sourdough sandwich created on the spot.

RIPE OLIVE
HERO SANDWICH

Split a long loaf of sourdough French bread. Hollow it out by tearing out soft center. Spread both cut surfaces with a large package (8 ounces) soft cream cheese. Brown thinly sliced ham (½ to ¾ pound) or canned luncheon meat in butter, and arrange on bread. Sprinkle with a can (2 to 4 ounces) of sliced or chopped ripe olives, drained. Bake in a hot oven (400°) for 10 minutes. Slice crosswise into large sandwiches. Makes 6 servings.

George Dwyer, Chief's Operator
Battalion District No. 5

In San Francisco, Italian restaurants with Italian chefs almost invariably have a "special" of spinach and eggs and hamburger—and the special takes the name of the restaurant. Probably Joe's was first: Supposedly, for lack of enough ground beef to make a "hamburger on the French (roll)," for some closing-hour customer, the chef composed Joe's special—of the things on hand. George Dwyer titles his special to honor another Italian restaurant; he usually makes it at the firehouse at the appropriate after-midnight hour.

Always French bread and butter with this.

BRUNO'S SPECIAL

1½ pounds ground chuck
2 large onions, chopped
1½ teaspoons salt
½ teaspoon coarsely ground black
   pepper
1 package (10 ounces) frozen chopped
   spinach, cooked and well drained
6 eggs, beaten
Parmesan cheese

In a large frying pan, brown meat slowly; when crumbly, add onions, salt,

and pepper, and sauté until meat is brown and onions limp. Stir in spinach, and heat through. Add beaten eggs, and continue cooking, stirring, until eggs are set. Sprinkle generously with Parmesan cheese. Serve immediately. Makes 6 usual servings, 3 firehouse servings.

George Dwyer, Chief's Operator,
Battalion District No. 5

Bob Hinman's unique trick to this sensational garlic bread is to actually "grate" the fresh garlic into the bread by rubbing it over the broiled-crisp cut surface of San Francisco's glorious sourdough French bread.

This is the likely plan for the bread part of the meal when Bob Hinman is cooking on a Wednesday or a Sunday—when it's San Francisco bakers' day off and he can't buy bread that's fresh from today's early-morning baking.

GRATED GARLIC
HERB BREAD

1 loaf sourdough French bread
4 cloves garlic
½ cup butter
Grated Parmesan cheese
Mixed dry Italian herbs
Paprika

Slice bread lengthwise, open, and place cut surfaces under broiler to dry out (not to brown). Peel and halve garlic cloves, and rub over cut bread surfaces to "grate" garlic into bread. Spread bread thickly with butter. Sprinkle with Parmesan, mixed Italian herbs, and paprika. Return to broiler until butter melts and topping browns slightly. Makes 12 to 16 servings.

Bob Hinman, Engine Company No. 26

Enchiladas are ubiquitous. They rate a special place in a fireman's heart. Everybody likes them. Everybody has an opinion on who makes them best. And nearly every cook has his own proud formula. There are hot enchiladas and mild ones; beef, chicken, meatless; of fresh, thick handmade tortillas or machine-made; old-fashioned, long, and complicated, or swiftly streamlined; cheesed with American, sharp Cheddar, Jack, or Parmesan.

Whatever the style, it's a special night when it's enchilada night—in firehouses all over the city. At serving time, nearly everybody gets into the act—with the main cook directing a big production line: One man dips tortillas, one spoons on sauce, one rolls, one puts on toppings, one adds Spanish rice—and off goes the hot Mexican platter to the long dinner table.

Captain Locke's formula is the long-time classic, passed along through firehouse generations, firehouses, and firehouse cooks for many years.

You can use machine-made tortillas, instead of the preferred handmade, but if you do, serve enchiladas as soon as they're made; if you try to hold them warm in the oven, the tortillas are likely to break. Accompany enchiladas with Spanish Rice (page 139).

CAPTAIN LOCKE'S ENCHILADAS

12 handmade corn tortillas

SAUCE

2 ounces dark Mexican chili powder
2 quarts cold water
2 tablespoons *each* salad oil and vinegar
1 can (8 ounces) tomato sauce
Flour mixed to a smooth paste with cold water
3 to 4 teaspoons cumin powder
Salt

Place chili powder in a large kettle, and stir in water, a little at a time, to make a smooth mixture. Stir in oil and vinegar, and heat to boiling. Stir in tomato sauce. Cook, stirring, adding enough flour-and-water paste to thicken to very thin batter consistency. Add cumin and salt to taste. Simmer for 30 minutes.

FILLING

1 pound lean Mexican chorizo sausages, cut from casings and crumbled

1 pound ground chuck
3 small onions, chopped
1 small can (4½ ounces) chopped olives
¼ pound grated dry Monterey Jack cheese
About 2 teaspoons cumin

In a large frying pan, brown chorizos and ground beef well. Add onions and sauté until limp. Stir in olives, cheese, cumin to taste, and enough of the sauce to moisten.

Choice of toppings: Grated dry Jack cheese, chopped onions, shredded lettuce.

To assemble: Dip each tortilla in sauce, put a spoonful of filling in the center, roll, place on hot serving plate, top with additional sauce, and serve immediately (or put into a warm oven to hold until serving time). Offer toppings. Makes 12 enchiladas, 6 servings.

Captain Arthur Locke,
Engine Company No. 37

This is known at the firehouse as well as in the Boccone household. At home, this pie is such a favorite it's been known to be hidden under a bed when company comes—out of sight, out of possibility of discovery.

This is a massive pie with a thick, peppered, eggy, rich and tender yeast-dough crust and a filling of spicy sausages and aged cheese bound with melting creamy cheese and eggs. Serve it hot or cold, in thin wedges, as a hefty *hors d'oeuvre*. Or serve fatter wedges hot, as part of a meal or for a late supper. Or take it cold on a wine picnic and carve it into sandwichlike wedges.

NAPOLETANA SAUSAGE PIE

1 cake yeast
¼ cup lukewarm water
8 cups flour
1 tablespoon salt
1 tablespoon coarsely ground black
   pepper
½ pound lard
1 dozen eggs, beaten
Peperoni filling
Egg white, slightly beaten

Crumble yeast into lukewarm water; stir to dissolve. Sift flour and salt into a large mixing bowl. Stir in pepper. With pastry blender or two knives, cut in lard until particles are fine. Combine eggs and yeast mixture, and stir into flour to form a soft dough. Turn out on a lightly floured board and knead thoroughly, until dough is soft and smooth. (Add no more flour than is necessary to keep dough from sticking.) Place in a greased bowl, cover, and let rise in a warm place for 4 to 5 hours or until doubled in bulk. Punch dough down. With a rolling pin, roll out slightly more than half the dough, on a lightly floured board, into a thick circle to line bottom and sides of a 12-inch heavy iron frying pan; fit into pan; arrange peperoni filling inside. Roll out remaining dough to a circle to fit top of pie; cut with a decorative vent; place on top of filling; flute edges to seal well. Place in a very hot oven (450°) and bake for 3 minutes. Reduce oven heat to moderate (350°) and bake 45 minutes more; brush top crust with egg white, and bake 15 minutes more or until deep golden. Allow to cool 5 minutes. Cut into wedges to serve. Makes about 24 appetizer servings, 12 to 16 larger servings.

PEPERONI FILLING

6 eggs, beaten
1½ pounds peperoni sausages, thinly
   sliced
1 pound Monterey cream or Teleme
   cheese, cut into small pieces
½ cup grated Romano cheese

Mix all ingredients together thoroughly.

Al Boccone, Engine Company No. 9

Bill O'Sullivan claims that Irish Bread came before Irish Soda Bread. According to O'Sullivan, the authentic old Irish bread is this version, made with milk and baking powder; later came the Irish soda breads, made with sour milk and soda.

One who might dispute that claim is Bud Madden, who bakes Irish Soda Bread (in firehouse lexicon: "Lump Bread") by a recipe he got from a friend's Irish mother who used to bake it in Ireland. So far, the controversy has not flamed into open dispute. And Irishmen's bread baking is too important at firehouses not to include both versions. (Bill O'Sullivan cools his loaf thoroughly before slicing. Bud Madden serves his while still warm.)

This recipe has been in the family for generations; "it came right from the old Irish sod."

BILL O'SULLIVAN'S IRISH BREAD

2 cups flour
½ cup sugar
3 teaspoons baking powder
½ teaspoon salt
2 teaspoons caraway seeds
½ cup raisins
2 eggs
½ cup milk
Additional milk and sugar

Sift together into mixing bowl the flour, sugar, baking powder, and salt. Stir in caraway seeds and raisins. Beat eggs with milk; gradually add to dry ingredients and stir thoroughly until mixture forms a sticky dough. Turn into a greased loaf pan (5 by 9 inches) and spread smooth. Drizzle a little milk over top of loaf and pat into dough; sprinkle generously with sugar. Bake in a moderate oven (350°) for 1 hour. Turn out of pan onto wire rack immediately; allow to cool thoroughly before slicing. Makes 1 loaf.

Bill O'Sullivan, Engine Company No. 5

This is tough-textured and rugged, and delicious with butter melting into juicy hot raisins and spicy caraway seeds.

LUMP BREAD

1 tablespoon soft shortening
½ cup sugar
2 cups buttermilk
½ teaspoon baking soda
2 tablespoons caraway seeds
1 cup raisins
4 cups flour
1 tablespoon baking powder
1¼ teaspoons salt
Butter

In a large mixing bowl, blend together shortening and sugar with a wooden spoon. Combine buttermilk, soda, caraway seeds, and raisins, and stir into sugar mixture. Sift together flour, baking powder, and salt, and gradually add to buttermilk mixture, beating with a wooden spoon. Beat well, and turn into a greased 9-inch heavy iron frying pan. Bake in a moderate oven (350°) for 1½ hours. Turn out of frying pan, wrap in a clean tea towel, and stand on end to cool for 30 minutes before cutting. Slice and serve with plenty of butter. Makes 1 loaf, about 10 servings.

Bud Madden, Engine Company No. 3

RAISINS

CHAPTER 14

desserts

DESSERTS

Firemen are dessert men when it comes to eating—but not so generally when it comes to cooking. It's rather a rare fireman-cook who is a general dessert-maker. But there are a few—and they are exceptional. And there are also those who have a single specialty.

Bob Burns says he likes to make sweet things because he likes to eat them. (But it must also be because he's so skilled. Even with a temperamental firehouse oven, he can make cream puffs so light they look like puffed golden clouds as they're stacked on the serving platter, powdered sugared, and almost bursting with softly sweetened whipped cream.)

He admits he always gets a lot of compliments with this splendid cheesecake and his warm apple torte served with ice cream.

Probably never was there a fireman who borrowed his wife's recipes who didn't take license with them: "The recipe says a half cube of butter for the crust, but why fool around with half a cube; I use the whole thing." The wife's version says to bake cheesecake 45 minutes. The husband says, "Bake it till it gets brown on top, maybe even an hour; it should be nice and stiff."

CHOCOLATE SHOT CHEESECAKE

CRUMB CRUST

1½ cups graham cracker crumbs
3 tablespoons sugar
1 teaspoon ground cinnamon
½ cup melted butter

Mix together thoroughly crumbs, sugar, cinnamon, and melted butter, and press over bottom and sides of a buttered 9-inch spring form pan. Bake in a slow oven (300°) for 5 minutes; cool.

CHEESE FILLING

2 large packages (8 ounces *each*)
  cream cheese, softened
½ cup sugar
1 teaspoon grated lemon peel
1 tablespoon lemon juice
½ teaspoon vanilla
2 eggs, separated

In a large mixing bowl, beat cheese until fluffy. Add sugar, lemon peel and juice, and vanilla; beat thoroughly.

Add egg yolks, one at a time, beating well after each addition. Beat egg whites until stiff but not dry, and fold in. Turn into crumb crust. Bake in a slow oven (300°) for 55 minutes or until golden and set.

TOPPING

1 cup sour cream
1 tablespoon sugar
1 teaspoon vanilla
Chocolate shot candy decorations

Mix together sour cream, sugar, and vanilla. Spread over top of hot cake. Return cake to slow oven (300°) and bake 10 minutes more. Cool thoroughly. Sprinkle top with chocolate shot. Remove sides from pan. Makes 10 servings.

Bob Burns, Truck Company No. 3

The texture is compelling—crusty on top, cakelike on the bottom, moist apple slices layered throughout. Bob Burns describes it as being "like apples in chocolate cake."

APPLE TORTE À LA MODE

4 tablespoons soft butter
1 cup sugar
1 egg
1 cup flour
1 teaspoon cinnamon
½ teaspoon baking powder
¼ teaspoon baking soda
⅛ teaspoon salt
3 apples, peeled, cored, and cut into lengthwise slices ⅛ inch thick
Vanilla ice cream

In a large mixing bowl, cream together butter and sugar. Add egg and beat until light and fluffy. Sift together flour, cinnamon, baking powder, soda, and salt into mixing bowl, and beat in thoroughly. With a rubber spatula or wooden spoon, gently stir apples into batter. Turn into a buttered 9-inch pie pan, and spread smooth. Bake in a moderate oven (350°) for 1 hour. Cool slightly. Cut into wedges while warm, and serve with ice cream. Makes 6 servings.

Bob Burns, Truck Company No. 3

Standing Ribs Delizioso, recipe page 47

Though called a pudding, it's really a deep-dish pie.

CHEESE-CRUSTED APPLE PUDDING

6 tart cooking apples, peeled and sliced
About ¾ cup sugar
About 1 tablespoon lemon juice
¾ teaspoon ground cinnamon
½ teaspoon ground nutmeg
Cream cheese pastry
Sugar

Toss together apples, sugar, lemon juice, cinnamon, and nutmeg; turn into a buttered baking dish (about 1½ quarts). Arrange cream cheese pastry over apples, turning under and fluting outside edges. Sprinkle lightly with sugar. Bake in a hot oven (400°) for 35 to 40 minutes or until crust is brown. Allow to cool partially. Spoon out to serve. Makes 6 servings.

CREAM CHEESE PASTRY

In a mixing bowl, stir together 1 small package (3 ounces) softened cream cheese and ½ cup soft butter. Mix in 1 cup flour. Gather into a ball, place between two sheets of waxed paper, and roll out to fit top of baking dish; cut decorative vents.

Bob Burns, Truck Company No. 3

GRAPE BLINTZES

2 small packages (3 ounces *each*)
   cream cheese, softened
1 cup small-curd cottage cheese
⅓ cup sugar
4 tablespoons golden raisins
2 teaspoons grated lemon peel
⅛ teaspoon salt
8 thin pancakes (recipe below)
Butter
Sour cream
Very finely chopped walnuts
Grape jelly

Mix together thoroughly cream cheese, cottage cheese, sugar, raisins, lemon peel, and salt. Spread center of each pancake with part of the cheese mixture. Roll up pancakes, folding in sides. Melt a small amount of butter in a frying pan; add pancake rolls, and slowly sauté, gently turning, until heated through and lightly browned. Top each with a generous spoonful of sour cream, a sprinkling of walnuts, and a small spoonful of jelly. Makes 8 dessert servings.

THIN PANCAKES

Beat 3 eggs slightly. Add 6 tablespoons flour and ⅜ teaspoon salt, and beat until smooth. Gradually add 1 cup milk, beating until batter is smooth. Heat butter (½ to 1 teaspoon for each pancake) over medium-high heat in 8-inch crêpe pan or shallow frying pan. Pour in about 4 tablespoons batter; quickly tilt and rotate pan so batter covers bottom. When lightly brown on bottom, turn and brown on second side. Makes 8 pancakes.

Richard Paganelli, Engine Company No. 17

VELVET DEVIL'S FOOD WITH COFFEE FUDGE FROSTING

2 squares (1 ounce *each*) unsweetened
    chocolate
½ cup soft butter
1 cup sugar
1 teaspoon vanilla
2 eggs
1½ cups sifted cake flour
1 teaspoon salt
¾ teaspoon baking soda
¾ cup ice water
Coffee fudge frosting

Melt chocolate over hot water; allow to cool. In a large mixing bowl, cream butter thoroughly. Gradually add sugar, and beat until mixture is thoroughly creamed and light and fluffy. Beat in vanilla. Add eggs, one at a time, and beat well after each addition. Blend in cooled chocolate. Sift flour with salt and soda; add to creamed mixture alternately with ice water; mix well. Turn into a buttered 9-inch square baking pan. Bake in a moderate oven (350°) for 30 to 35 minutes or until toothpick inserted in center comes out clean. Cool on a rack. Frost with coffee fudge frosting. Makes about 10 servings.

COFFEE FUDGE FROSTING

Combine in a saucepan 1½ cups sugar, ½ cup strong coffee, 1 tablespoon *each* light corn syrup and butter, and 2 squares (1 ounce *each*) unsweetened chocolate, cut up. Cover and slowly bring to a boil. Remove cover, and cook without stirring until a small amount dropped into cold water forms a soft ball (234° on a candy thermometer). Remove from heat; let stand until cool. Stir in 1 teaspoon vanilla. Beat until thick enough to spread. Quickly spread over cooled cake.

Frank Alianza, Engine Company No. 1

*Beer Buttermilk Pancakes,
recipe page 145*

Cold whipped cream melts into a soft cake with its own lemon custard sauce.

LEMON CAKE MacCARTHY

1¼ cups sugar
½ cup flour
¼ teaspoon salt
3 eggs, separated
Grated peel and juice of 2 large lemons
2 tablespoons melted butter
1½ cups milk
1 cup heavy cream, whipped

Sift 1 cup of the sugar, the flour, and salt together into mixing bowl. Beat egg yolks slightly, and stir into dry ingredients along with lemon peel and juice and butter. Add milk and mix thoroughly. Beat egg whites until foamy, gradually add the remaining ¼ cup sugar, and beat until stiff; fold into lemon mixture. Turn into an ungreased baking dish (about 2 quarts), set into a pan with hot water about 1 inch deep in bottom. Bake in a moderate oven (375°) for 30 to 40 minutes or until top is browned and knife inserted about halfway deep in center comes out clean. Spoon into serving dishes while warm. Top with whipped cream. Makes 6 servings.

Lieutenant E. L. MacCarthy,
Airport Company No. 1

Here's a smooth and simple dessert retired Lieutenant Hatzmier used to make on August nights, when fresh nectarines were in season.

TOKAY NECTARINES

6 large unpeeled nectarines, cut into
⅜-inch slices lengthwise
Sugar
Tokay wine

Put nectarines in a bowl, sprinkling with sugar to taste (about ⅓ cup total). Pour over them enough wine almost to cover (about ¾ cup). Cover and chill for 6 to 8 hours. Turn gently occasionally. Makes 6 servings.

Lieutenant Louis Hatzmier, Retired,
Engine Company No. 48

Frank Rey likes his Zabaglione chilled—and over fresh ripe figs.

GENOESE ZABAGLIONE

6 egg yolks
6 tablespoons *each* sugar and dry or
   medium Sherry
½ teaspoon grated lemon peel

Combine all ingredients in top of double boiler. Place over hot (not boiling) water and cook, beating constantly with wire whip or rotary beater, until fluffy and thickened, about 5 to 10 minutes. Chill or serve immediately in small stemmed glasses. Makes 4 servings.

Frank Rey, Engine Company No. 27

Ted Dal Broi bakes apples with an intensely fruity result—by baking the tartest of apples (green ones) and topping them with a biting sharp and sweet lemon sauce. Most firemen are great embellishers and top hot apples with hot sauce, *then* pour on heavy sweet cream.

BAKED GREEN APPLES AND LEMON SAUCE

4 large green apples
⅓ cup granulated sugar
¼ teaspoon cinnamon
Water
Lemon sauce
Heavy cream (optional)

Core apples; slit around center or pare upper third. Place in baking pan and fill cavities and sprinkle top with mixture of granulated sugar and cinnamon. Pour water ¼ inch deep in bottom of baking pan. Bake in a moderate oven (375°) for 45 to 60 minutes or until tender, basting occasionally with juices in pan. Serve apples hot, topped with hot lemon sauce. Pass cream. Makes 4 servings.

LEMON SAUCE

Combine ¾ cup unsifted powdered sugar and 1 teaspoon cornstarch thoroughly in a saucepan. Add grated peel and juice of 2 lemons and cook, stirring, over medium heat until slightly thickened and clear; stir in 3 tablespoons butter.

Ted Dal Broi, Truck Company No. 5

Red-Eye Pot Roast, recipe page 49

You could do this same dessert with peeled ripe fresh peaches instead of plums; use one large peach half for each serving.

FRESH PLUM BETTE

6 fresh ripe plums
Almond extract
Vanilla ice cream
½ cup heavy cream, whipped and lightly sweetened with sugar and flavored with almond extract
4 to 6 coconut macaroons, crushed into crumbs

Halve plums and remove pits. Place plums, cut side up, on broiling or baking sheet, and touch each with a drop of almond extract. Broil about 3 inches from heat until heated through. Place 3 plum halves, cut side up, in each of 4 stemmed dessert glasses or dessert bowls. Top each with a thin slice of vanilla ice cream, a spoonful of whipped cream, and a generous sprinkling of macaroon crumbs. Makes 4 servings.

Larry Middendorf, Engine Company No. 5

The nuts must be generous—and they must be walnuts.

PEACHES AND CREAM AND WALNUTS

For each dessert, put a chilled peeled fresh (or canned) peach half in a stemmed dessert glass. Center with a generous spoonful of seedless grapes. Sprinkle with chopped walnuts. Pour on cold heavy sweet cream.

Mel Lavoie, Engine Company No. 8

In the Mission district fire of September, 1964, the San Francisco Fire Department lost a great man and an excellent fireman.

Andy Benton is well remembered:

"He kept all his baking tools locked up in his locker."

"He'd say, 'I'll bake if you'll cook,' then proceed to pull out a little, yellowed, weathered slip of paper for a recipe, and go to work and turn out wonders."

"He was fast, too. He could whip out a pie faster than you could walk over to the store and buy one."

His apple pie was legendary. Great round sugared humps in the top piecrust promised the fat apple quarters inside.

ANDY BENTON'S APPLE PIE

6 medium-sized pippin apples, peeled, quartered, and cored
¾ cup sugar
1 teaspoon *each* ground cinnamon and nutmeg
Pinch of ground cloves
Pastry
1½ tablespoons fresh lemon juice
Additional sugar
3 tablespoons butter
About 1 tablespoon heavy cream or evaporated milk
Ice cream

Combine in a saucepan apples, ¾ cup sugar, cinnamon, nutmeg, and cloves; cover and cook over low heat, turning occasionally, for about 10 minutes, until sugar and spices form a syrup. Turn into pastry-lined pie pan. Sprinkle with lemon juice and additional sugar, depending on tartness of the apples (2 to 4 tablespoons). Dot with butter. Cover with top crust, cut with a decorative vent; flute edges to seal. Bake in a very hot oven (450°) for 15 minutes; reduce oven heat to moderate (375°), and bake about 30 minutes more or until crust is deep golden (if necessary, cover outer edge with a ring of foil to prevent overbrowning). Brush top of pie with cream, sprinkle with sugar, and bake 10 minutes more. Allow pie to cool slightly; then serve warm with ice cream. Makes 6 servings.

PASTRY

Sift together into mixing bowl 2 cups flour and 1 teaspoon salt. With pastry blender or two knives, cut in ¾ cup shortening (hydrogenated vegetable shortening or lard) until particles are the size of small peas. Sprinkle in 5 to 7 tablespoons ice water, and toss with a fork. Gather together to form two balls. Let stand 15 to 20 minutes; then roll out on a lightly floured board into two circles to make lining and top for 9-inch pie.

Captain Andy Benton, Deceased,
Truck Company No. 7

Ashley Hobson rolls his cheery blue eyes and declares that this dark and moist date pudding is so rich you don't need any topping on it. Then continues, as if logically, "We usually have it with whipped cream or ice cream."

DATE PUDDING

1¼ cups flour
¼ teaspoon *each* baking powder and
   salt
¾ cup chopped walnuts
1½ cups cut-up dates
1 teaspoon baking soda
1 cup boiling water
¼ cup soft butter
1 cup sugar
1 egg
Whipped cream or vanilla ice cream
   (optional)

Sift together flour, baking powder, and salt; stir in nuts. Sprinkle dates with soda, and pour boiling water over them; let stand. Meanwhile, in a large mixing bowl, cream together butter and sugar. Add egg, and beat thoroughly. Stir in flour and nuts. Add date mixture, and stir to mix thoroughly. Turn into a buttered 8-inch-square baking pan. Bake in a moderate oven (350°) for 45 minutes or until toothpick inserted in center comes out clean. Cool in pan and cut into squares. Serve with whipped cream or ice cream. Makes 8 servings.

Ashley Hobson, Engine Company No. 40

Veal and Sausage Brochette,
recipe page 63

Several of the better San Francisco restaurants make a specialty and show of banana fritters for dessert. Occasionally, so does Ed McGovern at Engine No. 32—with his own variation of several sugars.

TRIPLE-SUGARED BANANA FRITTERS

2 cups flour
3 teaspoons baking powder
1 teaspoon sugar
⅛ teaspoon salt
1¼ cups milk
3 tablespoons salad oil
3 egg whites, beaten until stiff but not dry
About 6 bananas, peeled and sliced diagonally into 1½-inch pieces
Oil for deep frying
Powdered sugar
Cinnamon sugar (½ cup sugar mixed with ½ teaspoon cinnamon)
Sifted brown sugar (mixed with a little ground nutmeg, if you wish)

Sift together into mixing bowl the flour, baking powder, sugar, and salt. Combine milk and oil and stir in. Fold in egg whites. Allow batter to stand for 15 minutes. Dip banana pieces into batter to coat, and allow excess batter to drip off. Drop into heated oil (375°) for deep frying. Fry on each side until rich golden. Drain for a moment on paper toweling. Transfer to hot serving platter. Sprinkle one third of the fritters with powdered sugar, one third with cinnamon sugar, and one third with brown. Serve hot. Makes 6 servings.

Captain Ed McGovern,
Engine Company No. 32

When the Santa Clara Valley apricots come into their short but abundant season in July, Dave Hinman bakes fresh apricot pies.

The apricots are spiced with cloves, the crust with cinnamon. The pies are cut while still a little warm—and sometimes get an à la mode treatment.

CLOVED FRESH APRICOT PIE

5 cups sliced fresh apricots
2 tablespoons lemon juice
About 1¼ cups sugar
2 tablespoons flour
⅛ teaspoon ground cloves
Pastry for double-crust 9-inch pie
2 tablespoons butter
Cream or evaporated milk
Sugar
Ground cinnamon

Sprinkle apricots with lemon juice. Combine sugar to sweeten, flour, and cloves, and mix lightly with apricots. Turn into pastry-lined 9-inch pie pan. Dot with butter. Cover with top pastry, cut with a decorative vent. Flute edges to seal. Bake in a hot oven (425°) for 30 minutes. Brush top crust with cream; sprinkle with sugar and very lightly with cinnamon. Return to oven and bake 10 minutes more, or until crust is golden brown. Cool on a wire rack. Makes 6 servings.

Dave Hinman, Truck Company No. 5

Both the Hinmans (Dave and Bob) are bakers, and both do splendid things with cream puff pastry. The éclairs are Dave's; the cream puffs, Bob's.

MOCHA ÉCLAIRS

Cream puff pastry (recipe following)
Coffee cream filling (following)
Mocha frosting (following)

Spoon cream puff pastry onto greased baking sheet, shaping into fingers about 1 inch wide, 4 inches long, and allow about 2 inches between for spreading. Bake in a hot oven (425°) for 15 minutes; reduce oven heat to moderate (350°), and bake for 35 to 40 minutes more or until golden brown. Remove to wire rack to cool. When cool, cut open, remove any filaments of soft dough, and fill with coffee cream filling. Replace tops. Spread tops with mocha frosting. Chill for 2 hours. Makes 10 to 12 éclairs.

CREAM PUFF PASTRY

Combine 1 cup water, ½ cup butter, and ¼ teaspoon salt in a saucepan and bring to a boil. Add 1 cup flour all at once; then beat over low heat until mixture leaves sides of pan and forms a mixture that does not separate (about 1 minute). Remove from heat; continue beating to cool mixture slightly, about 2 minutes. Add 4 eggs, one at a time, beating after each addition until mixture has a satinlike sheen.

COFFEE CREAM FILLING

Beat 2 cups heavy cream with 6 tablespoons sugar, 2 tablespoons very strong cold coffee, and 2 teaspoons vanilla until stiff.

MOCHA FROSTING

Stir together 2 tablespoons *each* melted butter, very strong coffee, and powdered cocoa. Gradually add about 1½ cups sifted powdered sugar, beating, until mixture is smooth and of spreading consistency.

Dave Hinman, Truck Company No. 5

Plank Steak Barbecue, recipe page 100

Bob Hinman likes to experiment. Once he read a recipe for walnut pie, tried it—and the resulting pie was so hard, the firemen cut it up and sold it for candy bars. But most of his experimentation turns out blissful results—as his almond pie and these big, handsome cream puffs prove.

BITTERSWEET ORANGE CREAM PUFFS

Cream puff pastry (see page 178)
2 cups heavy cream
6 tablespoons sugar
1½ teaspoons orange extract
Bitter orange chocolate frosting

Drop cream puff pastry in large mounds from a tablespoon onto greased baking sheet, allowing about 2 inches between. Bake in a very hot oven (450°) for 15 minutes; reduce oven heat to slow (325°) and bake for 25 minutes more or until golden brown. Remove to wire rack to cool. Beat cream with sugar and orange extract until stiff. Cut tops off cream puffs and fill with whipped cream. Replace tops. Drizzle on chocolate frosting. Makes about 8 large puffs.

BITTER ORANGE CHOCOLATE FROSTING

Combine one 1-ounce square unsweetened chocolate, melted, and 1 teaspoon melted butter. Blend in 1 cup sifted powdered sugar, 2 tablespoons boiling water, and 1 tablespoon grated orange peel. Beat just until smooth (not stiff).

Bob Hinman, Engine Company No. 26

Southern pecan pie changed to a Western nut pie—of almonds. You might like a scoop of coffee ice cream on the side.

ALMOND PIE

2 eggs
½ cup light brown sugar, firmly packed
1 cup light corn syrup
2 tablespoons *each* flour and melted butter
½ teaspoon *each* vanilla and almond extract
⅛ teaspoon salt
1½ cups sliced or slivered almonds
Pastry for single-crust 8-inch pie

In a mixing bowl, beat eggs well with a rotary beater, then beat in brown sugar, syrup, flour, butter, vanilla, almond extract, and salt. Stir in almonds. Turn into pastry-lined 8-inch pie pan. Bake in a hot oven (400°) for 15 minutes; reduce oven heat to moderate (350°) and bake 20 minutes more or until filling is set. Cool on a rack. Makes 6 to 8 servings.

Bob Hinman, Engine Company No. 26

Purist cook though he is, Bob Hinman doesn't scorn the convenience of a packaged cake mix to make these easy and rich fudge-tasting cookies.

CHOCOLATE CHIP CHOCOLATE DROPS

2 eggs
½ teaspoon baking soda
½ cup melted butter
1 package (19 ounces) devil's food
   cake mix
½ cup flour
1 small package (6 ounces) semisweet
   chocolate bits
⅔ cup chopped walnuts (optional)
Powdered sugar (optional)

In a mixing bowl, beat eggs with soda. Beat in melted butter. Stir in cake mix and flour, mixing until all ingredients are moistened. Stir in chocolate bits and nuts. Pinch off dough and form into balls a little smaller than a walnut. Place 2 inches apart on ungreased baking sheet. Place on rack above oven center. Bake in a moderate oven (350°) for 12 to 13 minutes. Remove to wire rack to cool. Sift powdered sugar over tops. Makes about 4 dozen cookies.

Bob Hinman, Engine Company No. 26

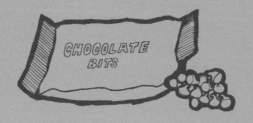

Chocolate Shot Cheesecake,
recipe page 161

Coffeecake is a dessert cake at Truck No. 5. Cut it into squares and serve it warm. It's a tender, tender cake with a sugared toasted-nut topping.

STREUSEL DESSERT COFFEECAKE

2½ cups all-purpose flour
1 cup brown sugar, firmly packed
¾ cup granulated sugar
¾ cup melted butter
2 teaspoons ground cinnamon
1 teaspoon *each* baking powder and
   soda
1 cup buttermilk
1 egg, beaten
½ cup chopped walnuts

Stir together in a large mixing bowl the flour, brown sugar, granulated sugar, butter, and 1 teaspoon of the cinnamon to make a crumbly mixture. Measure ¾ cup of the crumb mixture and set aside. Add to ingredients in mixing bowl the baking powder, soda, buttermilk, and egg; stir to mix thoroughly (mixture will not be smooth). Turn into a buttered 9-inch-square baking pan. Mix walnuts and remaining teaspoon of cinnamon with reserved crumb mixture; sprinkle over top of batter. Bake in a moderate oven (350°) for 45 minutes or until toothpick inserted in center comes out clean. Cut into squares. Makes about 8 servings.

Dave Hinman, Truck Company No. 5

When it's Christmas Day, the firemen on duty have a real Christmas dinner—a feast of many courses. Dick Breitbarth makes Steamed Christmas Pudding. He calls it "poor man's plum pudding," and serves it warm with a hot rum sauce or brandy hard sauce. (It's lighter than most plum puddings, and mildly spicy.)

The firehouse kitchen provides all the preparation equipment: a 2-pound coffee can (with holes punched in the lid or covered with several layers of foil tied on securely with string) for the pudding, a big kettle with a lid for steaming, a couple of coffee mugs placed on the bottom of the kettle for a steaming rack.

DICK BREITBARTH'S STEAMED CHRISTMAS PUDDING

1 cup grated raw potatoes
1 teaspoon baking soda
½ cup butter
1 cup brown sugar
1 cup grated raw carrots
1 cup raisins
1 cup chopped walnuts
1½ cups flour
1½ teaspoons cinnamon
1 teaspoon salt
¾ teaspoon *each* ground cloves and
   nutmeg

Mix potatoes with soda. In a large mixing bowl, cream together butter and brown sugar. Stir in potatoes with soda, carrots, raisins, and walnuts. Sift together flour, cinnamon, salt, cloves, and nutmeg into fruit mixture. Mix thoroughly. Turn into a buttered 2-pound coffee can (or 1½-quart mold). Cover tightly. Place on rack (or coffee mugs) in kettle with boiling water 2 inches deep in bottom. Cover and steam for 3 hours. (Add more boiling water to steamer as necessary.) Remove pudding from steamer; allow to stand 5 minutes before unmolding. Loosen at sides with a thin-bladed knife; gently tap out of can. Serve immediately. Makes 10 to 12 servings.

Dick Breitbarth, Engine Company No. 34

For lack of a better vessel, a cook at Engine No. 3 once threw the shortcake dough into a Dutch oven to bake. The rich-crusted results were so grand, it's now the custom.

A heavy frying pan or deep casserole will do at home.

DUTCH-OVEN STRAWBERRY SHORTCAKE

4 cups flour
½ cup sugar
2 tablespoons plus 2 teaspoons baking powder
1 teaspoon salt
¾ cup butter
4 eggs
½ cup milk
¼ cup soft butter
2 quarts strawberries, stemmed and sliced
About 2 cups sugar
2 cups heavy cream
¼ cup sugar
2 teaspoons vanilla

Sift together into mixing bowl the flour, ½ cup sugar, baking powder, and salt. Cut or rub in ¾ cup butter until particles are fine. Beat eggs with milk, add to dry ingredients, and mix thoroughly to make a soft dough. Turn out on lightly floured board and pat into a thick circle to fit bottom of buttered Dutch oven, heavy casserole, or frying pan (about 9-inch diameter). Bake in a moderate oven (375°) for 40 minutes or until deep golden. Slip onto wire rack to cool. Split into three layers; spread each with soft butter. Meantime, gently mix strawberries with sugar to sweeten; chill for 30 minutes. Whip cream with ¼ cup sugar and vanilla. To assemble, place bottom shortcake layer on serving platter, top with one third of the berries, and spoon on one third of the cream. Top with second shortcake layer, and repeat layering of berries and cream; repeat with third layer. Cut into deep wedges. Makes 10 servings.

Jack Sherry, Engine Company No. 3

Dutch-Oven Strawberry Shortcake